Has Archaeology Buried the Bible?

Has Archaeology Buried the Bible?

William G. Dever

William B. Eerdmans Publishing Company
Grand Rapids, Michigan

Wm. B. Eerdmans Publishing Co.
4035 Park East Court SE, Grand Rapids, Michigan 49546
www.eerdmans.com

Published 2020
Printed in the United States of America

26 25 24 23 22 21 20   1 2 3 4 5 6 7

ISBN 978-0-8028-7763-5

Library of Congress Cataloging-in-Publication Data

Names: Dever, William G., author.
Title: Has archaeology buried the Bible? / William G. Dever.
Description: Grand Rapids, Michigan : William B. Eerdmans Publishing Co.,
    2020. | Includes bibliographical references and index. | Summary: "A reeval-
    uation of biblical historicity, truth, and morality based on recent archaeolog-
    ical findings"—Provided by publisher.
Identifiers: LCCN 2019060216 | ISBN 9780802877635 (hardcover)
Subjects: LCSH: Bible. Old Testament—Antiquities. | Bible. Old Testament—Ev-
    idences, authority, etc. | Palestine—Antiquities. | Middle East—Antiquities.
Classification: LCC BS621 .D485 2020 | DDC 220.9/3—dc23
LC record available at https://lccn.loc.gov/2019060216

Contents

Preface

This book has been in the making for more than sixty years, since I was a young graduate student. I had been raised in the manse—one of a fundamentalist stance—and by that time I was myself a cleric while a student in a liberal seminary. Already I felt keenly the challenge of reading the Bible—especially the Christian "Old Testament"—intelligently, critically, yet in a way that did not compromise what I thought of as its enduring religious values.

I wrote an MA thesis on "Old Testament Theology," then in vogue. I went on to a PhD program at Harvard to pursue that interest with G. Ernest Wright, at the time one of America's leading Old Testament scholars and our most prominent biblical archaeologist. Archaeology soon won out over theology, and I began an archaeological career with Wright at biblical Shechem (Tell Balaṭah) in 1962. I never looked back. But I also never forgot my original aim: to help make the Bible more meaningful to modern readers. Now, however, I had a new pulpit, and perhaps in time a new gospel.

I have written numerous articles and books, most of them technical scholarly works on archaeology, some on biblical studies, all works for a rather small audience. This book, however, is meant to be different: truly popular, nontechnical, and unencumbered by copious footnotes and vast bibliography. It intends to simplify complex issues and take a commonsense, middle-of-the-road approach. Even though I have been a participant in nearly all the inevitable archaeological controversies over the years, I try to make the discussions here accessible and balanced, so I write in the third person.

Those who wish to pursue the issues treated of necessity rather simply here will find all the details and references to the vast literature in my *Beyond the Texts: An Archaeological Portrait of Ancient Israel and Judah* (SBL Press, 2017).

The list of Suggested Readings at the end of the book may also be helpful; it cites the best accessible and readable sources.

Some believers may think that I undermine the Bible, while secularists may say that there is no point in trying to save the Bible. I am doing neither. I only suggest a middle ground, an up-to-date but modestly optimistic approach to the Bible. Others may find this book moralistic; but the fundamental, universal issues are always moral. And the Bible, along with other great literature, remains a good guide.

I have become indebted to too many along the way to credit them all here: parents, teachers, family, students, and colleagues. My wife Pamela Gaber has listened to many trial readings and has offered improvements that I would not have thought of. An anonymous supporter and benefactor offered encouragement so strong that I had to write this book.

On a few technical matters, BCE and CE are used instead of BC and AD, in keeping with the most current usage. I use the Hebrew word "Yahweh" for God, since that is most often the actual term in the Hebrew Bible, not "Lord," as many translations have. "Yahweh" is the proper name of the national deity of Israel, best understood as the causative form of the Hebrew verb *hyh*, "to be," thus "He who causes to be," that is, the creator.

Translations from Hebrew may follow any one of several versions, and readers can compare on their own. Sometimes I provide my own translation or paraphrase. In all cases I try to convey the best meaning of the biblical text.

The land of ancient Israel is not called "Palestine," since that term came into use only later, in the Roman period, and in any case it is compromised by the current political situation in the Middle East. "Levant" is the more neutral geographical term, meaning modern Lebanon, Syria, Jordan, the West Bank, and Israel. "Southern Levant" includes the latter three. "Canaanite" is usually clear from the context. "Late Bronze Age" means the time period of circa 1500–1200 BCE; "Iron Age" from circa 1200–600 BCE.

I may use Arabic names for many biblical sites, usually large *tells* or mounds, because in some cases that is all we have, the ancient names having been lost.

The word "cult" is not derogatory but simply refers to religious *practices*, which is what archaeology illuminates best. I don't deal with theology directly, ancient or modern. I leave that to specialists, clerics, and others. Here I have no theological axe to grind. I also do not raise technical questions about the authorship or the structure of the biblical texts. That, too, is for specialists. But the text as it stands now is all we have to work with.

What concerns us here is not the question of who wrote the text or where or when, but rather what does it say, read in a straightforward way? In short, what did the biblical authors and editors think they were describing, and what did they mean? Then and only then will we proceed to a critical evaluation of the texts, using archaeology as a primary source. Thus, we can compare what the texts *did* mean, and what they may *still* mean.

Finally, biblical chronology is complex, so the dates here are those used by mainstream commentaries. Unless specified otherwise, they are all BCE. The word "Bible" always means the Hebrew Bible, often mistakenly called the "Old Testament" by Christians. Properly speaking, it is the Bible of ancient Israel and the Jewish community, today not old at all, but still current.

CHAPTER 1

Digging in the Dirt and in the Bible

The "Holy Land"—a fascinating, centuries-old concept—was about to take on new life when archaeological work began in the mid-nineteenth century in what was then called Palestine (modern Israel and the Palestinian territories), at the time part of the Turkish Ottoman Empire. Archaeologists had already begun making spectacular discoveries elsewhere in the Middle East, in Egypt and Mesopotamia, some promising to shed astonishing light on the Bible.

The first investigation of one ancient site in Palestine, however, came only in 1863, when Félicien de Saulcy claimed to have found the rock-cut tombs of the kings of ancient Israel (though they turned out to be nothing of the sort).

As actual excavations began in Palestine, and in Transjordan and Syria as well, in the late nineteenth and early twentieth centuries, the overriding goal continued to be to illuminate the long-lost world of the Bible. Thus, places chosen for excavation were typically sites known from the Old and New Testaments: Samaria, Megiddo, Jericho, and of course Jerusalem. The sponsoring societies were quite candid about their objectives. As the British Palestine Exploration Fund described itself in their initial statement in 1865:

> A Society for the Accurate and Systematic Investigation of the Archaeology, Topography, Geology and Physical Geography, Natural History, Manners and Customs of the Holy Land, for Biblical Illustration. (*Palestine Exploration Quarterly* 1 [1865]: 1–4)

Its sister organization, the American Palestine Exploration Society, founded in 1870, had an almost identical statement of purpose. But, significantly, to the goal of "illustration" it added "for the *defense* of the Bible." That would set the trend for American archaeology in Palestine for the next century.

Many scholars and members of the public in Europe were equally fascinated with what soon became an extended international effort to "prove the Bible." This effort was redoubled after the spreading challenge of late-nineteenth-
century "higher criticism" of the biblical text, which questioned the Hebrew
Bible's early date and essential historicity. By 1900, the proliferation of the
"heretical" modern views of the Bible had fueled the fierce "Fundamentalist-
Modernist" controversy, which soon divided virtually every major American
Protestant denomination (as well as Roman Catholic and Jewish groups). This
controversy about the "truth" of the Bible still shapes American religious and
even secular and political life to this day.

The literature of the time illustrates the heady early days of the biblical
archaeology movement. Melvin Grove Kyle, one of the editors of the evangel-
ical work *The Fundamentals* (which gave the controversy its name), declared
confidently in 1912:

> A flood of light is, indeed, pouring across the page of the exegete and the
> commentator and the critic . . . but the source of that light is neither criti-
> cism nor exegesis nor comment, but archaeology.[1]

In a 1933 volume titled *The Spade and the Bible: Archeological Discoveries
Support the Old Book,* one scholar exclaimed:

> Not a ruined city has been opened up that has given any comfort to un-
> believing critics or evolutionists. Every find of archaeologists in the Bible
> lands has gone to confirm Scripture and confound its enemies. . . . Not since
> Christ ascended back to heaven have there been so many scientific proofs
> that God's word is truth.[2]

Not until after World War I, however, did a specific school of "biblical
archaeology" emerge, founded by the legendary American archaeologist William Foxwell Albright and his followers, mostly biblical scholars and clerics.
Albright, in the field in Palestine himself from 1919 until the outbreak of World
War II, was certainly no fundamentalist. But he was fond of speaking of the expansion of fieldwork during this formative period as promising a "revolution"

1. Melvin Grove Kyle, *The Deciding Voice of the Monuments in Biblical Criticism* (London:
SPCK, 1912), 39.
2. The quotation comes from J. W. Newton, as cited in W. W. Prescott, *The Spade and the
Bible: Archaeological Discoveries Support the Old Book* (London: Revell, 1933), 19.

in our understanding of the Bible. In particular, his agenda was to demonstrate the historicity of the pivotal events in the stories of the Hebrew Bible.

These events were: (1) The migration of the patriarch and matriarch from Mesopotamia to Canaan in the early second millennium BCE; (2) the Hebrew exodus from Egypt and the conquest of Canaan ca. 1250–1150 BCE; (3) the giving of the law and the covenant with Yahweh, Israel's sole god, at Mt. Sinai; (4) the establishment of the united monarchy in the tenth century BCE under Saul, David, and Solomon, a "divine kingship"; and (5) the development of the nation of Israel and its religion and culture in the subsequent Iron Age as unique and under divine providence.

Albright's magisterial synthesis of his life's work was published in 1940 as *From the Stone Age to Christianity*. The latter development was obviously the fulfillment of the great evolutionary progress of civilization—Christianity, the Bible at its center, buttressed by archaeology.

Albright is long gone (he died in 1971), and all of his achievements have been undermined. The archaeological search for the historicity of the events in question has been all but abandoned. A revolution in viewing the Bible has indeed come, as we shall see in the following chapters, but hardly in the form that Albright envisioned.

Furthermore, the biblical archaeology movement underwent a collapse beginning around 1970. As archaeology progressed dramatically in Israel (the state of Israel having supplanted Palestine after 1948), both Israeli and foreign excavators were moving away from the uneasy alliance between archaeology and the Bible. Increasingly, this was seen as a liaison between archaeology and *theology*, and a particular American Protestant variety of Old Testament theology at that. The European and now the Israeli archaeologists never did readily embrace these ill-suited bedfellows. Unlike the Americans, few had been biblical scholars, much less clergy; certainly the Israelis were not rabbis. Thus by the mid-1980s, the old-style biblical archaeology had reinvented itself as a self-conscious, separate, and secular branch of Near Eastern archaeology.

The reborn discipline, much more professional and specialized, was first styled "Syro-Palestinian" archaeology (to broaden it beyond the immediate world of the Bible in Israel). But in view of the political realities in the region, the preferred name has become "Levantine" or "Southern Levantine archaeology," or simply "the archaeology of Israel" or "of Jordan" (now excluding Syria). The biblical texts are still considered important, but only when assessed separately and critically, and even then only as secondary sources for archaeology and history writing.

As promising as the new archaeology was initially, its "coming of age" rep-

Revisionism

All good historians are revisionists in the sense that they revise and rewrite history as new data become available. Recently, however, a group of mostly European Old Testament scholars have been so influenced by postmodern notions of "deconstructing" texts that they have advanced quite radical views. They suggest that no real "history" of Israel can be written because the biblical texts—their only source—are fictitious and therefore unreliable. The extremes to the right and left have polarized much biblical scholarship between "minimalists" and "maximalists."

A more productive course might be to steer between radical modernism and radical postmodernism, if that is still possible. Science and technology, democracy and capitalism, the unquestioning belief in progress—they all have flaws and limitations. But we must find something to put in their place.

See also "Postmodernism and the Western Cultural Tradition" (p. 140) and the selected readings on postmodernism in the back of this book.

resented a painful alienation from its venerable parent, the Bible. After all, from archaeology's beginning in the mid-nineteenth century in the Holy Land, its essential value for many had been to validate the history of events narrated in the Bible as the *ground of faith*. And Israel's faith, as well as that of modern believers, was understood to mean acceptance of the biblical writers' theological interpretation of the "meaning" of certain *real events*. Thus the declaration of biblical theology, ancient and modern, was construed as the *Magnalia Dei*, "the recital of God's mighty acts in history."

G. Ernest Wright, at the same time America's foremost archaeologist *and* Old Testament theologian in the 1950s and 1960s, had once declared: "In biblical faith, everything depends upon whether the central events actually occurred."[3] But what happens if the "central events"—patriarchal migrations, Moses and monotheism at Sinai, exodus and conquest, Israel's unique ethnogenesis—had not occurred? That was the crisis that post-biblical secular archaeology seemed to face. But how to resolve it?

Meanwhile, by the 1990s, confidence was failing, not only in the former biblical archaeology, but also in the Bible itself, especially the Hebrew Bible. Several scholars, particularly biblical revisionists in Europe, often called "min-

---

3. G. Ernest Wright, *God Who Acts: Biblical Theology as Recital*, Studies in Biblical Theology 8 (Chicago: Regnery, 1952), 126-27.

imalists," were arguing that the biblical texts were too late (Persian or Hellenistic) and too tendentious (Jewish propaganda) to be historically reliable.

While they rarely acknowledged it, these radical, skeptical biblical scholars were heavily influenced by mid- to late-twentieth-century postmodern thinkers in Europe. The assertions of the latter could double for those of the biblical revisionists: "there are no facts, only interpretations"; "there is nothing outside the text"; "one must have incredulity toward all metanarratives" (the Bible being of course the principal metanarrative); and "all claims to knowledge are merely social constructs."

Such nihilism makes writing *any* history impossible, since that task depends on evidence, on demonstrable facts. The skepticism was epitomized in a 1997 volume of essays (none by archaeologists or American scholars) entitled *Can a "History of Israel" Be Written?* The answer of most contributors was "no." There was nothing envisioned that would approach what most historians would call a real history—only a "history of the history," of the *myths* of biblical literature.

Granting the presuppositions of both classes of minimalists, we would be at an impasse in both historical archaeology and in the history of any real "Israel" in the Iron Age (ca. 1200–600 BCE). But could there be a middle ground between the extreme left (the Bible *cannot* be "true") and the extreme right (the Bible *must* be "true")? And if so, is it archaeology—an alternate and more innovative approach—that might be our best hope? Moreover, beyond the historical concern of "what happened?" there is a more urgent and universal question: "what does it *mean*?"

History and History Writing

Our English word "history" derives from Greek *historein*, "to inquire," that is, of past events. One common definition is that of the Dutch scholar Johann Huizinga: history is "the intellectual form in which a civilization renders account to itself of its past."

History is thus essentially storytelling, presuming of course that the stories are true—that they purvey a reasonably accurate account of what really happened in the past. From the time of the Greek historians Herodotus and Thucydides (and also the prior time of the composition and editing of the Hebrew Bible), history was only storytelling, often with some evidence provided for a core narrative of actual events, but often freely interpreted, artfully embellished, exaggerated, and even shamelessly (?) invented. But from the eighteenth century CE onward, in keeping with Enlightenment ideals of reason, history became an academic discipline where some objectivity and documentation of facts is taken for granted.

In keeping with our attempt here to address both questions, we must first show how archaeology as a *primary* source for history writing, one moving beyond the biblical texts, can write new and better histories of ancient Israel. Next we must demonstrate that what is left of ancient Israel in our "secular history," even though perhaps diminished in theological authority, can nevertheless uphold essential moral and ethical values.

We shall argue that henceforth archaeology will be central to the task of writing our own revisionist histories of ancient Israel, thereby occupying and holding the necessary middle ground. But if so, how do we defend the notion that the archaeological data are "primary" evidence in contrast to the biblical texts? The argument is that these data are primary by offering contemporary eyewitness information, whereas the biblical accounts were often written centuries later than the events that they purport to describe. Furthermore, the archaeological data, when they first come to light after being hidden for centuries, are unbiased. That is, they are unedited, in contrast to the biblical texts, which have been edited and reedited for twenty centuries or more.

Finally, the archaeological data are more varied and dynamic, expanding constantly on knowledge of things like the daily life of ordinary individuals and other subjects about which the biblical writers are simply uninterested, particularly women's lives.

Archaeology gives a voice to those countless generations of anonymous and forgotten folk in ancient Israel. It allows them to speak to us of *their* faith, and in doing so it can tell us why that faith may still matter. In the future, an intelligent, critical, modern reading of the Hebrew Bible will be possible only by considering the light shed on it by archaeology. That approach, and only that, will save the Bible from becoming obsolete, being dismissed as simply a curious relic. And not only will sophisticated secular humanist readers benefit, so will believers—at least those whose minds are open to new insights.

The following chapters will begin by summarizing the main events of the biblical stories, then evaluate them critically in the light of current archaeological evidence. Finally, we will show how a more balanced historical portrait of ancient Israel can still have maximum meaning in today's confusing world. That is why we archaeologists are not burying the Bible, but digging it up anew, for it is still a basic source.

We will demonstrate that new, critical readings of the Bible must be undertaken in the light of the new data. This may seem radical, since we must abandon many of the old literal readings, or else abandon the Bible altogether (which some may do). There is a middle ground, however, and that is to fall back on another traditional way of reading and comprehending Scripture, namely as *allegory*.

An allegory is "a literary or pictorial device in which characters stand for abstract ideas, principles, or forces, so that the literal sense has or suggests a *deeper* symbolic sense" (*American Heritage Dictionary*; italics mine). This way of reading is not intended to deny or to diminish the possibility of a literal reading, what Protestant reformers called "the plain meaning of Scripture." But instead of immortalizing a single meaning of profound literature—which the Hebrew Bible certainly is—this approach *transcends* simplistic interpretations in order to reach a higher, and hence more authentic, Truth.

There is nothing either new or radical about this way of reading the biblical texts. The Hebrew Bible already allegorizes itself. Biblical writers will cite an earlier assertion of the text in order to apply it to issues of their own day. This is what they say happened, but here is what it means "now." Thus during the monarchy, reformers declared that the meaning of the theme of Yahweh in the wilderness was to lead *them* to their promised land.

Later rabbis across the centuries did the same thing. The Torah was read with great respect, but the intent was always to penetrate to its deeper, spiritual meaning. And in the New Testament, Paul clearly allegorized the Hebrew Bible. Abraham, the man of faith, was the prototype of the Christian believer. Isaiah 7:14 was read as foretelling Jesus the Messiah, "born of a virgin," even though the text says nothing of the sort. This allegory rests not upon the actual text, but on a misunderstanding of the Hebrew word *almah*, "young woman," which had mistakenly come over into the Greek Septuagint translation (the Bible of the early church) as *parthenos*, "virgin."

Most allegories, however, begin with a correct reading of the original texts, in this case Hebrew, assuming that the text is not corrupt, although some are. James Kugel has written a magisterial introduction to rabbinical and early Christian uses of allegory, entitled *Traditions of the Bible: A Guide to the Bible as It Was at the Start of the Common Era*. Kugel shows that even before the Hebrew Bible had attained its final canonical form its stories, legends, songs, and prophecies had begun to be interpreted. Subsequently, each successive generation—especially the rabbis and later the church fathers—added their own insights into what became an authoritative reading. That was the Bible *plus* layers of interpretations adding new insights and meanings. As Kugel says:

> It was this *interpreted* Bible—not just stories, prophecies, and laws themselves, but the texts as they had, by now, been interpreted and explained for

centuries—that came to stand at the very center of Judaism and Christianity. This is what people in both religions meant by "the Bible."[4]

Of course Jewish and Christian allegories could differ. Song of Songs, for example, posed a problem. It was clearly an old, sensual, often erotic love poem, probably sung at weddings. It doesn't mention Yahweh, centering instead around two passionate and earthly lovers—the beloved bride and her ardent suitor. The book has no theological (or even moral) message. So why should it be included in the Bible? It almost wasn't, but Jewish interpreters decided that it was *really* about the love of Yahweh for his bride Israel. Not to be outdone, early puritanical Christians, equally uneasy, decided that the Song of Songs was *really* about the love of God for his people, the church. Without such allegorical interpretations, this book would never have made it into the biblical canon.

Later, allegorical interpretations, both Jewish and Christian, took on great authority. In the Jewish tradition, the Mishnah and the Talmud became in some cases *the* authoritative interpretation. The Mishnah (from the Hebrew *shanah,* "to repeat") is an extended commentary completed in the third century CE, arranged into six orders, which are in turn divided into tractates, 63 in all. The Talmud (from Hebrew *lamad,* "to learn, teach") has two versions, a Jerusalem one and a Babylonian one (in the diaspora). It comprises further commentary on the Mishnah, compiled in the fourth century CE. Then there are collections of midrash (from Hebrew *darash,* "to seek out"), oral and written traditions extending from 400–1200 CE. Finally we have numerous medieval commentaries, such as those by Rashi, Maimonides, and other famous rabbis and sages.

All this elaborate, ongoing Jewish commentary, spanning more than a thousand years, is based on the notion that the Torah—the most fundamental text—consists of the original written version plus the continuing oral tradition. The *whole* is Scripture. Ephraim Urbach, in his book *The Sages,* puts it this way:

> The expositions of the Sages possess decisive authority and deserve at least the *same place* in the scale of religious values as the written Torah, and in truth transcend it.[5]

4. James L. Kugel, *Traditions of the Bible: A Guide to the Bible as It Was at the Start of the Common Era* (Cambridge, MA: Harvard University Press, 1999), xix.

5. Ephraim Urbach, *The Sages: Their Concepts and Beliefs* (Cambridge, MA: Harvard University Press, 1987), 304–5, italics added.

Lawrence Schiffman, in *From Text to Tradition*, describes it as follows:

> This material became the new scripture of Judaism, and the authority of the
> Bible was now defined in terms of how it was interpreted in the rabbinic
> tradition. Scripture had been displaced by the Talmud.[6]

In the Christian tradition, the early church fathers and medieval commentators added their own interpretations to Scripture, both the Old and New Testaments. The Roman Catholic Church elevated the interpretations of bishops and popes to the point where they—not the biblical texts—became the effective dogma. Protestants in the fifteenth-century Reformation protested: *sola scriptura*, "back to the biblical text." But they, too, resorted to what theologians have called "pneumatic exegesis," "reading with the eyes of the spirit," that is, the Holy Spirit.

Are such allegorical or metaphorical readings of the biblical texts, as we propose here, legitimate then? They are indeed necessary if the biblical stories are not to be left to fundamentalists, who almost always miss the point in insisting there is only *one* reading—theirs. The fact is that great literature survives and is regarded as great precisely because it incorporates many *levels* of meaning. There is the original author's meaning, which is not necessarily monolithic. Then there is the response of early readers and interpreters, which may vary, and without which the text would never have been preserved. Then there are many layers of interpretation, over many centuries in the case of the Hebrew Bible, which by now has become Scripture, "holy writings." Sacred or not, that text requires interpretation, perhaps many interpretations if it is to remain timeless.

If there were only one correct interpretation of the Bible, that would have been agreed upon long ago. And we would not have such serious schisms within the Christian church (with more than three hundred Protestant denominations and sects); or a Judaism that has Orthodox, Conservative, Reconstructionist, and Reform branches.

It is all a matter of varying interpretations of one basic biblical text, acknowledged by all. For centuries there were no rules for such endeavors (called "hermeneutics") because there was no source of independent information beyond the text itself. The Bible stood in splendid isolation, a unique monument from antiquity. But within the past generation or so we have had, at last, an

---

6. Lawrence Schiffman, *From Text to Tradition: A History of Second Temple and Rabbinic Judaism* (Hoboken, NJ: Ktav, 1991), 287.

independent witness to the world within which the Bible first took shape—archaeology. That means that we have an unprecedented opportunity to craft new *authentic* meanings of the biblical narratives, relevant for our time, with no less authoritative moral imperatives. That is what this book attempts.

CHAPTER 2

Patriarchs, Matriarchs, and Migrations:
Where Is the Promised Land?

The Biblical Narrative

The story in Genesis of the migration of Israel's ancestors from Mesopotamia to Canaan, the "promised land," is well known (Gen. 11–12). It is essentially the prehistory of the Israelite people, as well as the foundation of their later claim to the land of Canaan during the settlement era and monarchy.

After the flood story in Genesis, Abram is introduced as a son of Terah, living in the city of Ur, presumably his homeland in southern Mesopotamia. Terah moves his family to Haran in Upper Syria, where he later dies. After his father's death, Abram, now a seventy-five-year-old man, has visions of Yahweh (later Israel's national deity), who commands him to take his barren wife Sarai, his brother's son Lot, and all their property and set out for a place that will be revealed to him. All the rest of the family left behind, Abram's little troop journeys to Canaan.

Yahweh's direction to Abram and his entourage to journey to distant Canaan—more than 1200 miles over land—is explained in the story in terms of God's intent to make of Abram and his descendants "a great nation" in its new homeland, uniquely blessed and recognized by all the other nations.

Abram and Sarai depart from Haran, arriving ultimately at Shechem, in the hill country north of Jerusalem (Gen. 12:6). There Abram receives an endorsement of the earlier promise of the land of Canaan as an inheritance for his descendants. Thereupon he builds an altar, presumably in thanksgiving. Abram then moves southward to Bethel, where he builds another altar and "invokes Yahweh's name"—a sign of his loyal obedience. Thus Abram's covenant with Yahweh and the promise of the land is sealed.

In Canaan, Abram's son Isaac is born, who then has a son named Jacob (also called "Israel" in a later text), who in turn bears twelve sons who are destined to

Canaan

The term *Cana'an* for a territory or an ethnic group in the Levant is thought to derive from Hurrian (Syrian) *kinahhu*, "purple-dyed cloth." The evidence is that the Canaanites and later Phoenicians were famed as merchants of costly dyed cloth for royalty or elite classes.

The word "Canaanite" as an ethnic designation first occurs in Mesopotamia ca. 1800 BCE, then as the name of a region or country in later texts. These and Late Bronze Age texts concerning the heyday of Canaan (ca. 1500–1200 BCE) are ambivalent about the exact territory, but the general geographic designations would have encompassed approximately modern-day Lebanon, Syria, Israel, the West Bank, and Jordan.

With the collapse of the Late Bronze Age ca. 1200 BCE, Canaanite culture disappeared, to be replaced by several other ethnolinguistic entities—early "Israel" among them.

become the ancestors of the twelve tribes of Israel. Thus the theme of "the patriarchs of Israel" is elaborated. Today we would add the "matriarchs of Israel": Abram's wife Sarah; Isaac's wife Rebekah; and Jacob's wives Rachel and Leah.

Abram and his family eventually settle at other sites in Canaan, in Mamre near Hebron; in Gerar and elsewhere; and notoriously in Sodom in the Jordan Valley (Gen. 13–23). During a famine, Abram makes a journey to Egypt and returns (Gen. 12:10–20). Jacob goes back to the land of Aram in Syria, where he finds his wives. Joseph, Jacob's son, is sold into slavery by his brothers and ends up in Egypt, where he eventually rises to the position of prime minister (Gen. 37–41).

The covenant with Abraham (whose name was changed in his old age; Gen. 17:5)—an "everlasting covenant" with his offspring "throughout their generations" (Gen. 17:7)—remains in place despite Joseph's setback. Next, Joseph's brothers and their father Jacob seek refuge in Egypt during another famine. They meet Joseph, are recognized and forgiven, and eventually settle in Egypt. Joseph too remains in Egypt, dies, and is buried there (Gen. 43–50).

That story is told to explain how the descendants of Joseph and his forebears, Abraham, Isaac, and Jacob, come to dwell in Egypt, and how after Joseph's death and loss of power they become slaves. There the patriarchal era ends, and the scene is set for the exodus several centuries later and the deliverance of the Hebrews from Egyptian bondage. With that, the prehistory of Israel that takes up most of the book of Genesis comes to an end.

Even before we turn to the external archaeological data, there are internal issues with the patriarchal stories in the book of Genesis. Some are moral issues. Abraham has sexual relations with Hagar, his wife's servant, who is a slave; and when Ishmael is born, both are abused and flee. Ishmael's descendants will be numerous, but they will be a pariah people. Abraham also has other slaves in his household.

When the king of Gerar, Abimelech, is attracted to Sarah, Abraham lies and says that she is his sister and is thus available. When she is seized, he is too cowardly to defend her, and he still insists that she is "really" his sister.

Lot is a ne'er-do-well who deserts Abraham and settles down in Sodom. When the inhabitants of Sodom come to Lot's house and demand that he bring out strangers ("angels" in the biblical story) to whom he has offered his hospitality so they can rape them, he refuses and offers his daughters instead. In another story, Lot falls into a drunken stupor, and his two daughters sleep with him and become pregnant.

One story about Abraham is difficult to rationalize on any grounds, because it appears to impugn the motives of both Abraham and Yahweh. That is the famous story of Yahweh's command that Abraham sacrifice his beloved son Isaac—the miracle child—as a bloody offering. The biblical rationale, of course, is that God was only testing Abraham's faith and unquestioned loyalty. But what kind of God would do such a thing? And what kind of father would willingly comply? Clerics and theologians have struggled for centuries to explain this story, but average readers will probably throw up their hands in despair.

Then there are the miracles. Abraham, a shepherd, rallies 318 fighting men from his household, goes up against a coalition of kings in Transjordan, defeats them, and pursues them all the way north of Damascus (Gen. 14). Angels come down from heaven and chat casually with humans. Sarah has a baby at the age of ninety. Such events may make for dramatic stories, but they are fictitious.

Apart from moral misgivings, there are a number of anachronisms in the Genesis stories that raise questions. Although the stories are apparently set in an early second millennium context, there are a number of references that betray the realities of the much later Iron Age. These include the mention of camels, which were only domesticated much later, and the presence of Philistines in Canaan, Arameans in Syria, and the Moabite and Edomite peoples and nations in Transjordan, all of which emerged only in the Iron Age. "Ur of the Chaldees"—Abraham's place of origin—is problematic since the term Chaldea for southern Mesopotamia (Babylonia) does not come into use before the seventh century BCE. In summary, even if the stories do contain some earlier components, they cannot have been composed and edited into their present form much before the end of the monarchy.

Finally, the overriding theological agenda of the patriarchal stories is transparent, and it compromises the stories' authenticity as history. Several of the stories in Genesis about individuals are clearly what we call "eponymous." That is, they are told to explain *later* names, in the author's day, by positing a remote theological ancestor. For instance, the bizarre story about Lot's daughters' sons of incest is told to introduce "Moab" and "Ben-Ammi," the fathers of Moab and Ammon, who would later become Israel's rivals and arch-enemies in Transjordan. We now know that these people did not emerge until centuries after the putative setting of the stories of Genesis.

The story of Jacob outwitting his brother Esau and stealing their father Isaac's birthright blessing is told to explain how Esau's descendants, the Edomites in Transjordan, later became Israel's enemies and were not to be blessed by Yahweh. Similarly, Ishmael, Hagar's son, is the eponymous ancestor of the later Arab tribes in the desert regions.

Much more to the point, a good deal of the cycle of stories about Jacob has to do with how his twelve sons became the ancestors of the later twelve tribes of Israel. Significantly, Jacob's name is changed to "Israel"—a dead giveaway to the motive of these stories.

All these stories reflect the geopolitical situation of the Israelite monarchy in the Late Iron Age, not any historical situation in the "age of Abraham." To be sure, these stories are set in an earlier theoretical context that may have some historical verisimilitude; but in their present form they are clearly fictitious. They justify ancient Israel's attempts at self-identification in her struggles with her neighbors. Israel, and she alone, is the chosen people.

An Archaeological Critique

The story of the patriarchal migration to Canaan, the promised land, looms large in the Hebrew Bible's epic story of Israel's fulfillment of her national destiny, so it was one of the earliest test cases for the biblical archaeology movement. Albright, in particular, summed the matter up in 1963:

> As a whole, the picture in Genesis is historical, and there is no reason to doubt the general accuracy of the biographical details and the sketches of personality which make the patriarchs come alive with a vividness unknown to a single extrabiblical character in the whole vast literature of the ancient Near East.[1]

1. W. F. Albright, *The Biblical Period from Abraham to Ezra* (New York: Harper & Row, 1963), 5.

Ethnography

Ethnography (from Greek *ethnos*, "people"; see also "Ethnicity" (p. 61) is one branch of the discipline of anthropology. Ethnography is the systematic study of ethnic groups (not "races") based on in-depth interviews of typical individuals by skilled observers, especially in the case of nonliterate societies.

In Levantine archaeology, the focus of ethnographic fieldwork is on the Bedouin of the region, comparing modern pastoral nomads with ancient peoples and lifestyles. The goal is to develop better research models.

See also "Postmodernism and the Western Cultural Tradition" (p. 140) and the selected readings on postmodernism in the back of this book.

G. Ernest Wright, another giant of the biblical archaeology movement, echoed his mentor's views almost as confidently in his textbook, *Biblical Archaeology*:

> We shall probably never be able to prove that Abraham really existed, that he did this or that, said thus or so, but what we can prove is that his life and times, as reflected in the stories about him, fit perfectly within the early second millennium, but imperfectly with any later period.[2]

Albright had dated the patriarchs to his Middle Bronze I period (ca. 2100–1900 BCE). He saw them portrayed in the Genesis stories as tent-dwellers, pastoral nomads who traversed great distances in their seasonal migrations, then ultimately settled down in Canaan. Thus the patriarchs were to be understood in terms of typical Middle Eastern bedouins. So the ethnographic parallels were instructive. Moreover, Albright saw his Middle Bronze I archaeological period as one that followed the near-total collapse of urban life in the Early Bronze Age, when people reverted to a pastoral lifestyle to survive. In that case, the stories of the biblical patriarchs would fit perfectly then, and in no other archaeological period, since the Middle Bronze I was unique.

Wright, however, would move the patriarchs down slightly later, into the Middle Bronze II era, now dated ca. 1800–1500 BCE. But the question remains: are there any actual *dates* in the biblical texts that would fit with these, or any other periods, in the archaeology of Israel?

Biblical chronology is notoriously complicated and inexact, since the ancient writers had no fixed dates, and only a few rough correlations with sup-

2. G. Ernest Wright, *Biblical Archaeology*, revised edition (Philadelphia: Westminster, 1962), 40.

posed historical events in their own time, themselves undatable. To make a long story short, if we compile a series of biblical synchronisms, we might calculate that Abram left Ur for Canaan ca. 2091 BCE. The biblical chronological scheme would then work out this way, based on the assumption that Solomon's death occurred ca. 930 BCE, five years before the well-documented raid of the Egyptian pharaoh Shoshenq (1 Kgs. 14:25):

2091 BCE	Abram's departure for Canaan
1876 BCE	Jacob's descent into Egypt
1446 BCE	Exodus from Egypt
966 BCE	Construction of Solomon's temple, 480 years after the exodus, in his 4th year, assuming that he ruled 40 years (1 Kgs. 6:1; 11:42)

The date of 2091 BCE would correlate closely with the date of Albright's Middle Bronze I period, ca. 2100–1900 BCE. But the biblical dates cannot be relied upon, for many reasons. For one thing, the date for Abram depends

Archaeological Periods

Archaeologists employ a sort of shorthand to describe and characterize a stratum in a mound or a historical and cultural horizon. Thus we may argue over whether the evidence for early kingship in ancient Israel is "Iron IIA" or "Iron IIB," and we debate when such a transition occurred. Not only is this confusing for nonspecialists, it begs the question of historicity. What we all want to know is, when in real time did these events happen? After all, we invented these labels, so they are nothing but conveniences (or inconveniences). Yet some labels are essential if we are to classify and discuss anything.

So which labels will we use here for the relevant periods? Here is our preferred scheme, somewhat simplified:

Middle Bronze I	2000–1800 BCE
Middle Bronze II	1800–1650 BCE
Middle Bronze III	1650–1500 BCE
Late Bronze I	1500–1300 BCE
Late Bronze II	1300–1200 BCE
Iron I	1200–1000 BCE
Iron IIA	1000–900 BCE
Iron IIB	900–700 BCE
Iron IIC	700–600 BCE

upon the Bible's date of ca. 1446 BCE for the exodus from Egypt, which we now know cannot have been earlier than ca. 1200 BCE. And Albright's Middle Bronze I date is ruled out for other reasons. While the patriarchal stories in Genesis do seem to portray a pastoral nomadic lifestyle, and in some detail, according to the archaeological evidence the sites of Shechem, Hebron, Beersheba, and Gerar do not exhibit any occupation in Albright's Middle Bronze I period (now known as Early Bronze IV). Furthermore, the Middle Bronze I or Early Bronze IV period can no longer be characterized as *entirely* pastoral nomadic. We now know of a number of permanently settled agricultural villages and even some small towns—but significantly not the ones named above in the biblical stories.

There are indeed many aspects of the patriarchal narratives in Genesis that correspond to the way in which historians and ethnographers describe bedouin or pastoral nomadic lifestyles, ancient and modern, in the Middle East. There are even striking details in the biblical stories that suggest that the biblical authors did not simply invent these events. Either they were dealing with real historical persons and events, or at least they had some authentic sources.

Among numerous features of the biblical narratives that seem to reflect pastoral nomadic lifestyles, the following may be noted.

1. The patriarchs are highly mobile; they live not in houses, but in tents.

2. They are not farmers, but herders, dependent for their livelihood on flocks of sheep and goats and transporting their goods on the backs of camels (or donkeys).

3. They migrate in stages over long distances, never staying long in one place, searching for pastureland and water for their herds. They live along the fringes of the Fertile Crescent, frequenting the semi-arid pasturelands between the great desert and the settled agricultural zone. They may bury their dead while on the trek in isolated cemeteries (for instance, Abraham's burial of Sarah in a purchased cave).

4. They have some knowledge of towns and cities along the way, but for the most part they avoid relationships with urbanites and regard their lifestyle as inferior and threatening (compare the Sodom and Lot narratives).

5. The mobile group is large and consists of several kin-based, closely related, multigenerational families, each headed by a sheikh-like patriarch. Polygamy is typical. The hierarchical organization suggests that we are dealing with tribes and clans that are not distinct ethnic groups, but are one part of an indigenous "dimorphic" society. These peoples

comprise a different socioeconomic component—the rural and pastoral nomadic element, rather than the more agricultural and settled urban element.

6. Despite some necessary degrees of tribal solidarity in order to survive, there are rivalries and even armed clashes between groups, especially over pasture and water rights, as well as family and tribal heritage (Abraham's wars with the eastern tribes in Genesis 14). Treaties may be struck in attempt to resolve these conflicts.

7. One way of maintaining family stability and enhancing status is reflected in elaborate rituals of hospitality (Lot entertaining the "angels").

Granted that many of the elements of the Genesis narratives reflect the realities of pastoral nomadic lifestyle, we shall note presently that such stories could fit *anywhere* in the history of the Middle East, even today.

Wright's proposed date in our Middle Bronze II period, in the early second millennium BCE, fares somewhat better. That is the general era in which we meet a group of Mesopotamian pastoral nomads known as Amorites and remembered in the Hebrew Bible as closely related to the original Canaanite inhabitants. The groups of people known in our texts as Amorites appear in Mesopotamia first ca. 2500 BCE and gradually become predominant. The term *amurru* in Akkadian, the local language of Mesopotamia, denotes "westerners," that is, western in contrast to the eastern Semitic peoples of Mesopotamia. The Amorites probably originated somewhere in the steppelands of Syria, in the Jebel el-Bishri or Palmyra region. As mobile pastoralists, they gradually infiltrated the settled regions to the east, where they were initially regarded as intruders. Cuneiform texts describe them as barbarians who have no homes but wander aimlessly about, who subsist on wild crops, who do not know how to behave in a civilized manner, who do not even bury their dead.

These Amorite nomadic groups become a menace when they increase in number and begin to move with their flocks into the settled zones. Thus the urban authorities first oppose them directly, even building a wall to keep them out. Then they try to co-opt them by forcibly settling them in certain restricted zones, taking a census, and giving them some semiautonomous status. These Amorites are still somewhat migratory, but the authorities keep meticulous records of their movements and monitor them carefully.

In time, however, these foreign elements in Mesopotamia become ever more sedentary. Some settle in towns and become merchants, go-betweens intersecting between tribes and townspeople, some even rising to become mayors. By the eighteenth century BCE, the Amorites are so thoroughly acculturated (if not assimilated) that both the Assyrian kings in the north and the Babylonian kings in the south are of Amorite extraction and proud of it. The great Babylonian king Hammurabi is an Amorite. And the famous Assyrian King List begins with "the seventeen kings who lived in tents."

It was the well-documented sedentarization of the West Semitic Amorites that led scholars like Albright and others to see in that mid-third to mid-second millennium process the historical background in which to understand the migration and settlement of the patriarchs in Canaan. Abraham, then, was considered an Amorite tribal chief.

How are we to explain the way in which the biblical stories of the patriarchs took shape and found their way into the biblical narrative as the prologue to the story of Israel's destiny in the land of Canaan? As we have shown, the biblical writers do not necessarily relate specific and well-attested historical events. These are *composite* stories that may contain some authentic-sounding features here and there. But they do not fit into any one period, nor do they revolve around only one consistent theme. In any case, these foundation myths about the ancestors of Israel designated those who were destined to become the chosen people in their chosen land.

The fact that these are not entirely fantastic tales, even though written centuries later, that they include many plausible details, should not surprise us. After all, large pastoral nomadic segments of the population have been characteristic of the Middle East for at least the last ten thousand years, and their bedouin descendants are still around and visible to this day. Most authorities estimate that the perennial percentage of nomadic elements of the population of most ancient societies was around ten percent.

Simply put, the biblical writers set their imaginative tale of supposed pastoral nomadic origins into the context of the nomadic lifestyles of their *own* day, with which were thoroughly familiar. And what better way to enhance the odyssey of a people from relatively obscure beginnings to becoming a great nation?

We know that groups of West Semitic peoples, Amorites and others from Mesopotamia related to the Israelites linguistically and possibly ethnically, did make their way even farther afield. They moved from Canaan into the Egyptian delta in the early- to mid-second millennium BCE, when they became known as "Amu" or "sand dwellers." One colorful wall painting from a nineteenth- to eighteenth-century-BCE tomb at Beni Hasan depicts a party of thirty-seven distinctly garbed Asiatics entering the delta, trading *kohl* (eye shadow) and possibly copper. One even wears a "cloak of many colors," possibly like Joseph's. At the site of Tell el-Dab'a in the Nile delta, a large, early second millennium settlement has been excavated, where the houses, tombs, and pottery are all nearly identical to the material culture of ancient Canaan in this period. All this would seem to resonate with stories of the patriarchs' descent into Egypt.

What is more fascinating is the fact that another group of Semitic people known as the Hyksos also migrated to Egypt, in this case during the interregnum known as the Second Intermediate period (ca. 1650–1550 BCE). During the Fifteenth Dynasty they rose to power as foreign kings in the delta. Two or three of the six known names of these Hyksos rulers are demonstrably Semitic. One king is named Jacob-Har, the exact equivalent of the biblical name Jacob, which is probably an abbreviation for Jacob-Har, meaning "may the mountain god (Har) protect" (or possibly Jacob-El, "may El protect"). All this would seem to provide a possible historical context within which a Semite from Canaan named Joseph could actually have become a high-ranking official—an otherwise implausible story, given Egypt's well-known xenophobia.

The Joseph tale had a long life. The Roman-period Jewish historian Flavius Josephus actually made a specific connection between Joseph and the Hyksos kings. He postulated that the new pharaoh "who did not know Joseph" (Exod. 1:8) was Thutmosis III, the Eighteenth Dynasty king who finally ended the Second Intermediate period ca. 1480 BCE and expelled the hated Hyksos. That correlation would help to explain why the remaining Semites in Egypt ("Hebrews") eventually ended up as slaves. Might Josephus have had an ancient source on Egyptian history that has been lost to us?

Other lines of extrabiblical evidence have been sought in order to date the patriarchs and thus to fix them in a believable archaeological and historical context. Here the search is for parallels, archaeologically attested social and economic institutions in the ancient Near East. First, Albright and others noted that in the eighteenth-century-BCE cuneiform archives from the site of Mari on the Euphrates (mentioned above) there are detailed descriptions of the aforementioned Amorites who bear obviously non-Mesopotamian personal names. These names include typical "sentence-names" relating the individual to a patron deity. Examples would be Shamshi-Adad ("the god Hadad is my sun") or Yasmah-Adad ("Hadad makes me rejoice").

The patterns of these names are closely related to many patriarchal names. Thus Jacob is an abbreviated version of Jacob-El, a West Semitic name that means "may El (the god) protect." Joseph probably represents an Amorite-style name like Joseph-El, "may (the god) El make me increase" ("El" being one of the names of God in the Hebrew Bible).

The Documentary Hypothesis

Since the mid-nineteenth century, biblical scholars have come to view the composition of the Hebrew Bible as much more complex than traditional Jewish and Christian scholarship had thought. The revolution was brought about by applying the methods of literary criticism, especially the comparison of various ancient literatures based on the Enlightenment ideal of the primacy of reason.

The result of such literary criticism of the Pentateuch was to distinguish several "schools" responsible for different sections of the text:

J: a source using the name "Yahweh" ("Jahweh" in German) for God, from the ninth century BCE

E: a source using the name "Elohim" for God, from the eighth century BCE

D: a source best seen in the book of Deuteronomy, from the seventh century BCE

P: a priestly source, responsible for most of Leviticus but also many narratives elsewhere in the Pentateuch, from the sixth century BCE

Thus the "JEDP" school of biblical interpretation was born. The attribution of the entire Pentateuch to these four sources—known in sum as the Documentary Hypothesis—remains influential today. Many of the details of the theory have been aggressively challenged, but the underlying idea that different scribal groups in different eras contributed to the text we have today continues to dominate biblical scholarship.

There are also Amorite tribal names that are similar to those of the twelve tribes of Israel. Thus at Mari we meet the *binū yamina* ("sons of the south," i.e., the southern tribe). That would correspond to the tribe of Benjamin in the Bible.

Possible socioeconomic parallels from a later period were also found at the site of Nuzi, on the upper Tigris River. Cuneiform texts from the fifteenth to fourteenth centuries BCE mention practices that seem to be reflected in some of the Genesis narratives. For instance, a Nuzi marriage contract permits a barren wife to give a slave woman to her husband so as to produce children and heirs. That custom reminds one of Abraham's wife, Sarah, giving her maid Hagar to Abraham as a surrogate mother (Gen. 16:1–4). Another Nuzi custom allowed a man to adopt a son and make him a legal heir, as Abraham attempted to do with Eliezer, an Aramean from Damascus (Gen. 15:2–4).

When the above parallels were first discussed, they seemed persuasive. But the Mari and Nuzi texts are some three hundred years apart. And now we know that these and many other parallels that we could cite span at least a thousand years in ancient Near Eastern history, so none of these parallels provide a specific date for the biblical story. And in any case, similarities do not constitute proof.

The main chronological problem, however, lies in the biblical texts themselves. After a century and a half of critical analysis of the Pentateuch, or the "five books of Moses," mainstream scholars are largely agreed that we have a combination of four separate sources or literary traditions. They are designated J and E for the names used for God in many narratives, Yahweh ("Jahweh" in German, where the designation originated) and El; D, for the bulk of Deuteronomy, considered to be the product of the "Deuteronomistic" historian who compiled the whole and added the book of Joshua–Kings; and P, the priestly source (as in the book of Leviticus). The patriarchal accounts are the work of the J and E editors, but these stories were usually preserved in oral tradition and thus could not have been written down before the ninth or eighth centuries BCE at the earliest, when writing became widespread. So the version we have is anywhere from four hundred to twelve hundred years later than the events it purports to describe. Given what we now know from archaeology and other sources, these are *composite* stories. They contain some, perhaps many, authentic events, but these events are telescoped so that the final version does not fit into any specific timeframe except for the Israelite monarchy, when the stories were finally committed to writing.

To be sure, many written documents from the ancient Near East can be shown to rest on older oral traditions, which may have been preserved for centuries with surprising accuracy. But when one looks at the incredibly detailed stories in Genesis—like the genealogies with dozens and dozens of individual names, or the Sodom and Lot epic—one is inclined to be skeptical. How could such complex plots and details have been remembered accurately for many centuries? What then is the most likely way for a thoughtful reader to view these biblical narratives?

What Is Left and Does It Matter?

First, a critical, sophisticated reading does not mean simply dismissing the biblical stories as fantastic and therefore fictitious. They are not "fantastic" at all, since extrabiblical evidence shows that they have at least a general historical and cultural context within known second-millennium-BCE cultures in the ancient Near East. So, however fanciful some specific features may seem, it is clear that these stories were not simply invented out of whole cloth.

The authors had some authentic sources at their disposal, both oral and written, some perhaps quite early. They were not charlatans, deliberately deceiving readers, nor were they naïve. But they were also not modern historians, intent upon being factual and objective. Such histories are dependent on modern notions of historiography, which do not antedate the eighteenth century.

The original biblical writers and their early editors were essentially storytellers, as all ancient historians were (think of the Greeks). And their stories were told and retold around campfires, in village homes, in courts of kings, cherished for centuries (even now) because they enshrined *moral values* that are timeless and universal—recognizable, everyday human values—even when the stories are mystical tales about the gods and eternity. In short, the patriarchal stories and many other stories in the Bible are what literary analysts and historians of religion call "myths." But look beyond our natural apprehension. Myths must not be dismissed as fairytales that modern, sophisticated readers can only ridicule. Myths are *profoundly* true, in the sense of "metaphor"—literally something "beyond" the ordinary, the obvious (Greek *metapherein*, "to transfer").

A myth is a readily understandable way of communicating a larger-than-life truth, of saying something about a reality almost beyond words. A myth is a symbol (another Greek word, from *symballein*, "to throw together"). A symbol is a simple, concrete expression that attempts to represent the ineffable, the *ultimate* reality. The cross or the star of David are symbols. A flag is only a symbol. Are these things true? Of course, profoundly so.

Myth

The word "myth" derives via Latin from the Greek *mythos*, meaning "story." But myth is not, as many believe, a fictitious story to be dismissed as irrelevant or uninstructive. A myth is simply a narrative, usually an ancient story, about the supernatural or larger-than-life legendary heroes. Myth is an attempt to provide a story—a worldview—capable of explaining *why* things are the way they are.

Many of the Bible's stories are best understood as myths. Take, for example, the garden of Eden story. No critical reader understands the narrative as historical. Yet when read with sympathy and imagination, it is a profound portrait of human nature—flawed but full of promise. Mythmaking characterized all ancient societies of which we have any knowledge. But we moderns also make our myths, and they make us.

But can something that is not literally true be persuasive? Can fiction teach us anything of value? The easy answer comes with more questions. Are Shakespeare's plays devoid of ethical and moral content because they are obviously fiction? Or think of the ways we often teach small children how to behave by telling them nursery rhymes. Little Red Riding Hood wasn't real, but the story is true insofar as it teaches children not to go out alone for a walk in the woods. Perhaps more to the point for biblical readers, the parables of Jesus (and of many rabbis, ancient and medieval) are not "true" stories, as everyone knows. But they are *metaphorically* true, and thus universal in their appeal. The prodigal son came home and was redeemed.

One may surmise that some of the original readers (or hearers) of the biblical stories may have understood them as metaphorically true. After all, sophisticated or not, these people were not fools; they could recognize and enjoy a "tall tale," and they could find a meaning they could live with.

The fact is that the deepest and most profound mysteries of human life and destiny are mediated to us not so much by prose, but by poetry. That is why the patriarchal stories, even if largely metaphorical, nevertheless ring true for many, as they have from the beginning. These imaginative tales are told not simply for their undoubted human drama, much less to write a believable history, but because their writers wanted to tell us and all their readers *what really matters*. The writers felt free to elaborate on the sources they had, even to invent some details to flesh out their story, because they had a larger moral objective in mind. For them, the "history" they were writing was His-story. They gave us a marvelous account of how Yahweh had acted decisively in their own history, then added an interpretation that gave meaning to these events.

These are didactic stories, designed to teach us what we need to know to get on with life, to be fully human. That is why they are immortal—true in a profound sense that we instinctively grasp.

So where is the *real* promised land? And how can we venture there? If we read the patriarchal epic with a sympathetic imagination—with insight into its deeper meaning—the promised land is here and now. It is wherever and whenever we discover who we are, where we came from, and where we are going, together with our ancestors, to fulfill our common human destiny in this world.

The promised land is not on any map, but is etched on our hearts and minds by giving us a vision to live by. The founding fathers (who knew Scripture well) saw America as the "New Israel," the land of promises yet to be fulfilled, a dream and a destiny. To read the stories of the patriarchs and matriarchs of ancient Israel with a plodding literalism is to miss the point. These remarkable, memorable stories are about origins and identity; about taking risks; about necessary losses; about daring to set out for the unknown; about the journey being more important than the destination; about life as faith, rather than knowledge; and finally about what it is to be fully human, to be true to nature and our species.

In summary, the question is whether the historical "core" of the Bible—what is left after archaeology has helped to separate fact from fiction—can still be morally edifying. Archaeology in the last generation or so has forced upon us new readings of biblical stories like those of Israel's patriarchs and matriarchs. There can be no turning back to the innocence of our parents or of our youth; we know too much. That means that if we moderns are not to reject the Bible altogether, we must learn to read it with new eyes; with a fresh imagination; with a combination of wide-eyed faith and cynicism, of knowledge and wisdom, belief and unbelief.

We archaeologists have indeed provoked a crisis for believers by introducing hard facts that challenge the simplistic readings of the Bible. The Bible *is* historical, but it reads more like a historical novel. It is authentic in the sense that the places and the plot are realistic, the players are like real-life characters from a certain time, but the book is fiction—believable fiction. If we archaeologists have forced new readings, we also point the way ahead, because in digging up a more *realistic* ancient Israel, we are not burying the Bible. We are bringing it to life again—not only for believers, but for any readers who believe that we can and must learn from the past.

CHAPTER 3

Yahweh versus Pharaoh: Holy War

The Biblical Narrative

The biblical account of a miraculous exodus from Egypt and a dramatic military conquest of all Canaan is spelled out in detail principally in the books of Exodus, Numbers, Deuteronomy, Joshua, and Judges. The story constitutes a substantial portion of the literature of the Hebrew Bible, and it covers what is regarded as the formative period of Israelite history. It is a story of origins, of self-identity, and of national destiny. But is it historically true? A lot depends on how we attempt to answer that question.

Despite the length of the biblical narrative, the events can be easily summarized. The Hebrews had been enslaved in Egypt for some 430 years (i.e., since Joseph's day). They were now reduced to poverty and misery, their lives threatened by unending violence. Miraculously, Moses appears as their savior—raised like a prince in Pharaoh's court, but at heart a Hebrew.

Galvanized by anger at seeing an Egyptian overlord beating a Hebrew slave making bricks, Moses kills the Egyptian. He then flees for his life to the wilderness, the land of Midian, where he has a vision of a strange deity in a burning bush. This god is called "Yahweh" in the text. Moses responds, but at first he does not know the god's name. He insists upon hearing it and is told that the name of the deity is something like "I am the one who creates" (which is roughly what Yahweh means in Hebrew). Then Yahweh further identifies himself as "the god of Abraham, Isaac, and Jacob," whereupon he reaffirms the promise of the land of Canaan.

Despite his misgivings, Moses is reassured when Yahweh miraculously turns his staff into a snake and back into a staff again. He appears before Pharaoh to demand, "Let my people go!," but Pharaoh's heart is hardened and he only makes the slaves' conditions harsher.

Ten horrible plagues follow: things like runaway frogs; lice; cattle disease; a bloody Nile; floods and hailstorms; locusts; an eclipse of the sun; and finally, the sudden death of every firstborn Egyptian male child. This is the hand of Yahweh raised against Pharaoh. The Hebrews are forewarned of the final plague, and by smearing lamb's blood over the doors of their houses they ward off the nighttime visit of the Angel of Death (an event later commemorated in the Passover feast). Pharaoh is utterly devastated, and he relents: "Go! Take everything with you!" Thus the exodus from Sinai to Canaan begins.

What the Bible describes in the book of Exodus as a "mixed multitude" goes forth. They are said to number 600,000 fighting men, plus women and children. The Egyptians pursue them, but their chariots are swept away when, after the Israelites miraculously cross the Red Sea on dry land, the waters flood.

The Hebrews journey on through the Sinai to dozens of sites, led by a cloud during the day and a pillar of fire by night. They are sustained by feeding on wild quails; by gathering "manna," evidently a breadlike substance on bushes; and by finding water springing from the rocks.

Eventually the Hebrews camp at Mount Sinai. Moses ascends the mountain, where Yahweh dictates the Ten Commandments to him. When he returns to the camp, he has an elaborate tentlike "tabernacle" built to house the two tablets upon which the Ten Commandments are written. Then Moses charges the assembled people with Yahweh's legal and ritual demands (as elaborated further in the books of Leviticus and Deuteronomy).

The Hebrews, however, are unfaithful to the covenant. They rebel, with the result that Yahweh condemns them to sojourn at the oasis of Kadesh Barnea, in the eastern Sinai, for thirty-eight years until the wayward generation dies off. Only then will they be allowed to resume their journey. Already the Hebrews are said to be organized in a confederation of twelve tribes. The book of Numbers documents their ritualized movements en masse through Transjordan, where they defeat king after king and destroy many sites. They acquire flocks and cattle, and some even settle down. The levitical priests oversee their ritual activities and ceremonies under Moses's leadership, especially the Passover. The people become frustrated and restless, but Moses reassures them.

Eventually the Hebrews arrive at Mount Nebo, overlooking the promised land, with a magnificent view of its expanse and its riches. But Yahweh informs Moses that he will not be allowed to enter the land (presumably because of occasional mishaps in Sinai). Joshua, already noted for his military prowess, will succeed him. Moses dies at the age of 120, his powers unabated, and he is buried by Yahweh in the land of Moab.

Sometime later the Hebrew tribal confederation draws up on the eastern bank of the Jordan river, opposite Jericho, the gateway to the promised land. Joshua pauses to send out spies to do reconnaissance, but they come back to report that the Canaanite cities stand on high hills and boast formidable city walls. Nevertheless, following Yahweh's promise of victory, Joshua devises a plan.

The Israelite troops surround the city, marching around it in a show of force for six days. On the seventh day, they march around the city seven times. They blow a great blast on trumpets, and the mighty walls of Jericho come tumbling down. The victorious Israelite forces burn the city and slaughter all the inhabitants, even killing the animals. No loot is taken for personal gain, only some silver, gold, and cult vessels for their own sanctuary. The conquest of the land of Canaan has begun.

The book of Joshua documents the conquest in meticulous and breathless detail. It is a celebration of Yahweh's holy war against all who, like Pharaoh, dare to oppose him. There are three lightning-like, successful campaigns, the first pushing inland from Jericho to the central hill country of Canaan. The set piece there is the conquest of 'Ai at the head of the valley leading up to Jerusalem. A force of some three thousand men goes up against the walled town, but they suffer heavy casualties and are driven back. Joshua despairs of ever conquering the Canaanites, but Yahweh explains that the Israelites were defeated because they defied his command of *herem*, "total sacrifice." They discover that Achan had earlier taken some of the loot that was devoted to Yahweh. After Achan confesses, he, his sons and daughters, and even his livestock are stoned to death and their bodies burned. Thereupon, the Israelites attack again, and this time they finish the job. Twelve thousand inhabitants of the city are slain.

The site of 'Ai—the name of which in Hebrew means "ruin heap" (likewise the modern Arabic name: *et-Tell*)—remains as a permanent witness to Yahweh's vengeance upon his enemies. Gibeon, the next site, is spared, because it surrendered and sought mercy. The lessons of holy war had been learned. The rest would be commentary.

There ensues a rapid campaign to the south, where again the incoming Israelites are overwhelmingly victorious. The Israelites vanquish all the Canaanite cities, destroying "all who breathed" (Josh. 10:40). They win again and again because "Yahweh, the God of Israel, fought for Israel" (Josh. 10:42).

The story then shifts to the north, where the Israelites seize Hazor, "the

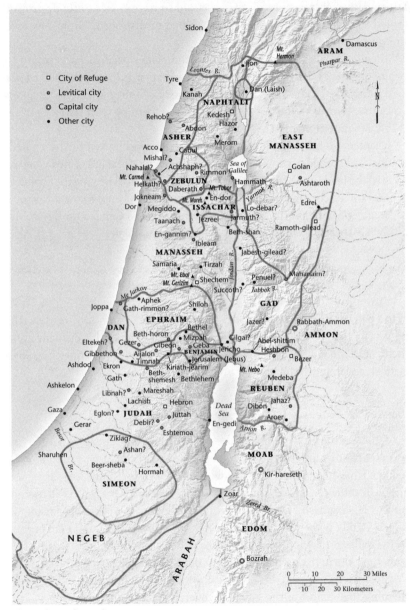

The Tribes of Israel

head of all those kingdoms" (Josh. 11:10). They burn the city to the ground and execute the king (Josh. 11:10–11). All the other cities in the north are then taken. Although not burned, they are said to have been utterly destroyed, looted, and their inhabitants evidently killed or displaced. "So Joshua took the whole land" (Josh. 11:23).

Then Joshua distributes the land, now completely pacified, apportioning it out among the twelve Israelite tribes. Joshua chapter 12 lists in chart-like form all the destroyed Canaanite cities and their kings—thirty-one in all. Chapters 15–22 then parcel out the territories and cities according to the Israelite tribes that are to inherit them.

Chapters 22–23 are two long addresses given by Joshua to the tribal confederation. The second occurs at Shechem, the first city Abraham visited when he entered the land long before. This is a farewell address, renewing the covenant at Sinai and celebrating the fulfillment of Yahweh's promise to the forefathers of Israel. The long pilgrimage from Mesopotamia, to Canaan, to Egypt, and ultimately back to Canaan—the Holy Land—is complete.

An Archaeological Critique

If the patriarchal narratives pose some problems for modern readers, the books of Exodus, Numbers, and Joshua constitute a minefield. Virtually every incident in the biblical narrative as summarized above raises questions for a critical reader, much more so for archaeologists.

The Biblical Exodus

First, there is the problem of the date of the biblical account as we have it. The books of Exodus and Numbers belong to the Yahwist and Elohist strands of the Pentateuch, which, as discussed above, are dated to the ninth to eighth centuries BCE at the earliest. The book of Joshua, however, is part of the Deuteronomistic History, also discussed above. This magisterial, unified epic history of Israel extends all the way to the fall of Jerusalem in 586 BCE, and even beyond to the exile in Babylon, and it must have been compiled in its first edition sometime late in the monarchy, that is, the late seventh century BCE.

Most scholars equate this historical work (often abbreviated "DtrH") with the long-lost "scroll of the Law" discovered in the temple in King Josiah's day—perhaps planted there by orthodox parties—which became the basis for sweeping Yahwistic reforms (2 Kgs. 22:8–11).

Another way of dating the exodus story in the Bible would be to look at demonstrably Egyptian elements in it. Thus the names of Moses, as well as the Hebrew midwives Shifrah and Puah, are not Semitic but Egyptian. The story of Joseph and Potiphar's wife resembles the Egyptian "Tale of Two Brothers." On the whole, however, the distinguished Egyptologist Donald Redford has argued that the exodus story fits best in the Saite period of Egypt, in the seventh century BCE. That would correspond closely with the date suggested above for the Deuteronomistic History.

In any case, the exodus and conquest stories in their present form (the only one we will ever have) are some four to six hundred years later than the events that they purport to describe. Once again, there is the problem of sources, both oral and written traditions, as discussed above. To be sure, "late" does not necessarily mean "fictitious," as the biblical revisionists we have already met opine, but the distance does urge caution.

Then there is the question of the date of the events themselves. Working again with the notoriously difficult biblical chronology, we would arrive after several synchronisms at the date of 1446 BCE for the departure of Moses from Egypt. Traditionalists have long regarded that date as fixed. But all current scholars, including evangelicals, have accepted the fact that the only archaeological horizon in which our Israelites (or "Proto-Israelites") could have emerged in Canaan is the late thirteenth to early twelfth century BCE.

The evidence for sweeping changes in settlement patterns, demography, ethnic self-identity, and material culture fit there, and nowhere else. This period represents the transition from the end of the homogeneous Late Bronze Age Canaanite culture to the fragmented early Iron Age in the twelfth to eleventh centuries BCE. It is then that several petty principalities (not yet states) arise, like Israel, the Philistine cities, the Phoenicians, and Ammon and Moab in Transjordan. They follow in the wake left by the wholesale collapse of the Bronze Age cultures throughout the eastern Mediterranean world. Nature abhors a vacuum; so does history.

We are fortunate in having a priceless extrabiblical text from this horizon, centuries earlier than the biblical texts and devoid of any biblical bias. It is the famous Victory Stele of Pharaoh Merenptah, the son and successor of Ramesses II (the pharaoh of the exodus, though not mentioned in the Bible). Merenptah ruled from ca. 1213–1203 BCE, and that general date is significant because it marks the first time in history that "Israel" is mentioned in any text. Moreover, the stele differentiates Israel as unique among other peoples in Canaan in constituting "a people" (with a distinct ethnic marker in the text) rather than a state or city-state. Here is one translation of the poem:

Plundered is Thehenu; Khatti is at peace;
Canaan is plundered with every evil;
Ashkelon is conquered;
Gezer is seized;
Yanoam is made nonexistent;
Israel is laid waste, his seed is no more;
Kharu has become a widow because of Egypt![1]

It is worth noting that the Egyptian text never alludes to any Israelite people as escapees or hints of revenge. Merenptah claims that he has wiped out Israel *in Canaan*. "His seed is not" turns out to be an idle boast, but the Egyptian intelligence on which the Victory Stele was based got most of it right. There was an Israelite ethnic group—not yet a state-like entity—somewhere in the hill country of central Canaan around 1200 BCE. And it was well enough known to the Egyptians to have been considered a threat.

Skeptics have downplayed this inscription, but it tells us a lot—all that we need to know at the moment. But how had such an "Israel" gotten to Canaan and gained a foothold there? Does the Bible really explain that? If it does not, can archaeology, our only other source, help?

Having set up the problem of an exodus and a conquest, let us look now at the archaeological evidence. The crucial pieces of the puzzle have come together only in the last twenty-five years or so, so many of the handbooks are obsolete.

First, nothing like the biblical exodus is mentioned anywhere in the numerous Egyptian texts that we have. Of course, one can argue that the Egyptians could hardly be expected to admit to such an ignominious defeat. The Egyptian pharaoh is not mentioned by name in the biblical texts, although we now know that he could only have been the great Ramesses II, who ruled for sixty-six years (1279–1213 BCE), one of the most celebrated pharaohs ever. Asiatic slaves may have run away now and then during his reign, but hardly a throng of some three million, as the biblical text implies (above).

The Hebrew slaves are said to be making bricks in the store cities of Pithom and Rameses (Exod. 1:11). These sites have actually been located, and indeed they were occupied in the required period. The city of Rameses is to be identified with the extensive remains at Tell ed-Dab'a and Qantir in the eastern delta. Asiatic slaves had been numerous in Egypt for hundreds of years. In one Egyptian inscription, one is shown being beaten while making mudbricks

1. Translation following Anson F. Rainey and R. Steven Notley, *The Sacred Bridge: Carta's Atlas of the Biblical World* (Jerusalem: Carta, 2006), 99.

by none other than Ramesses himself, so this part of the exodus story is not necessarily fantastic. But a full-scale slave uprising is.

The miracles wrought by Yahweh through Moses are crucial to the biblical story of escape from Egyptian bondage—especially the famous ten plagues that finally brought Pharaoh to his knees. Scientists have frequently tried to explain these plagues and other miracles on a rational basis. For example, hailstorm; cattle disease; locusts; lice; and a red, muddy Nile that can look bloody can always be said to be natural disasters. The crossing of the Red Sea on dry land might be explained by postulating a great tsunami that could have parted the waters (though the Hebrew text reads the "Reed Sea," the location of which, if any, is unknown). And the "pillar of fire" in the Sinai wanderings could have been the orange smoke cloud emanating from the explosion of the volcano on Santorini (ancient Thera), which was once dated around 1450 BCE, almost exactly the old date of the exodus. (Though that explosion is now dated ca. 1650 BCE.) All these scientific explanations, however, miss the point: these are *miracles,* acts of God that cannot *be* explained; otherwise they wouldn't be miracles.

The one plague that defies any explanation, especially a theological one, is the slaughter of all the innocent Egyptian firstborn male children. No amount of rationalization can account for the behavior of such a capricious, cruel deity. This was mass murder, not just vengeance on Yahweh's supposed rival Pharaoh, but death inflicted on the entire population of Egypt. Such a horrifying tale cannot be morally edifying; it must be rejected by any reasonable reader.

The story of the Israelites crossing the Red Sea is problematic apart from the stupendous miracles involved. The Hebrew term *yam suf* does not mean "Red Sea," since the Bible does not use the word for "red," which would be *adom.* The term *suf* was mistranslated in the later Greek and Latin versions. A more literal meaning of the Hebrew term is "Reed Sea." Yet, despite biblical references to its location (such as Exod. 14:2), no such shallow crossing of the waters has been located or makes much sense.

After crossing the Reed Sea, the horde of two or three million Hebrews sets out on foot across the Sinai, that "great and terrifying wilderness." The borders of Canaan lie more than 150 miles away. The number is calculated from the 600,000 adult fighting men in the biblical account (Exod. 12:37). When adding women, children, and adolescent males, this would amount to as many as three million people. Attempts have been made to understand the Hebrew *elef,* "thousand" as meaning rather "hundred," thus reading six thousand, or even six hundred. But that is a counsel of despair—another attempt to explain the unexplainable.

The problem is that anyone who has ever traversed the Sinai and camped there (as I have) knows that the vast arid wastes of the desert could not possibly have supported even a small, straggling band of a few hundred—certainly not for thirty-eight years. Even the few thousand modern bedouin in the Sinai barely manage to survive. The biblical story, read literally, is simply not credible. In the wilderness itinerary (Exod. 20–40; Num. 1–33) much of the narrative is taken up with ritual commands, tribal allotments, various side trips, etc. Dozens of sites are mentioned, plus more than thirty in Transjordan mentioned in Numbers 33 alone.

Archaeologists have searched diligently to identify and locate any of the Sinai desert sites, especially when the Israelis held the Sinai after the 1973 war. Only two can be located with any confidence. Migdol, near the beginning of the journey (Num. 33:7), has been identified with Tell el-Borg, near the east bank of the Nile and the modern canal. It was an Egyptian border fortress during the time in question, hardly a place for wanderers to camp, even in small numbers.

Mount Sinai is crucial to the story, since that is where the Ten Commandments are said to have been given and the covenant with Yahweh promulgated. Numerous attempts have been made to identify this site, in the Sinai desert, in the Negev desert in Israel, and even in southern Transjordan. These are all fanciful suggestions, however, since we have no supporting data of any kind. One site, Har Karkom, in the Negev desert of Israel, is patently absurd, as are the others found by amateurs in Saudi Arabia. As is well known, the traditional site of Mount Sinai has been located at St. Catherine's monastery. But that tradition is not earlier than the sixth century of the common era, and in any case, it was originally based simply on guesswork.

Kadesh Barnea is the site where the Hebrews were said to have been held up for thirty-eight years, certainly enough time to have left substantial remains, especially for a large group. This site is clearly to be located at a small oasis near 'Ain-Qudeis in the eastern Sinai, the Arabic name *Qudeis* preserving the Hebrew name *Kadesh*. The site was extensively excavated by Israeli archaeologists when they held the Sinai, keen to establish a connection with the biblical story. On the small *tell* or mound, however, there are only three superimposed forts, dating respectively to the tenth, the eighth, and the seventh centuries BCE. Earlier than that, there are no structures, only a scattering of sherds. At most, a few stragglers passed this way in the late thirteenth or early twelfth century BCE.

One could, of course, argue that the vast numbers of Israelite settlers were located at some nearby small oasis. But no traces of such remains have been

Cultural Memory

One of the most common catchphrases of modern Old Testament scholarship is "cultural memory." It stresses how a text or body of texts, particularly ancient ones, come to form narratives (or even "metanarratives").

Whether these "stories from the past" are true is often not seen as important, nor can it be determined. The question is not "what actually happened?" but "how does this story *function* as it has come to be remembered in the culture?"

Memory is a critical factor in cultural formation. Otherwise literature like the Hebrew Bible would have long been forgotten. But memories are not simply snatched out of thin air; they are based on facts, even if exaggerated. Thus one can write at least a provisional history, in this case of an "Israel" in the Iron Age.

See also "Postmodernism and the Western Cultural Tradition" (p. 140) and the selected readings on postmodernism in the back of this book.

found anywhere nearby. The most likely explanation is that the site became an important Israelite pilgrimage site early in the later Iron Age (eighth century or so), when the Hebrew Bible was taking shape and the writers knew of the fort there. This is, again, "cultural memory," which can invent as well as discover truths.

The Biblical Conquest

When the Hebrews reach the southwestern borders of Canaan, they decide to avoid the southern coastal plain, because the Philistines are said to be settled there. So they turn eastward, across the northern Negev desert, to Transjordan. There, in what is southern Jordan today, they encounter the Midianites, a tribe to which Moses's father-in-law, Jethro, a tribal priest, belonged.

Moses had originally fled there to escape Pharaoh's wrath, and there he may have learned of a deity named Yahweh. Egyptian texts of the thirteenth century BCE describe a seminomadic tribe there called the "Shasu," who venerated a god named "Ya," no doubt equivalent to Yahweh. This is the only time that the divine name occurs for certain outside the Hebrew Bible.

Oddly enough, the Hebrews later take revenge on the Midianites and slaughter the king and all the males. When Moses learns that they have spared the women, he is enraged. He orders them to kill all the women as well, at least those with children; the virgins are for the taking (Num. 31:1–18).

When the Hebrew forces move north, several great victories are claimed, notably at Heshbon and Dibon (Num. 21:25–35). Biblical Heshbon is clearly to be located at the site with the Arabic name of *Hesban*, a few miles south of

Destruction Layers

The strata, or superimposed occupation layers, in a *tell*, or mound, can sometimes be separated on the basis of "destruction layers." These are stratigraphic horizons that are characterized by features like collapsed buildings, quantities of broken pottery and other objects, burn layers and ash deposits, and often evidence of looting, which may be followed by abandonment.

These destruction layers, however, may be restricted to a small portion of the mound, and do not necessarily imply a wholesale destruction of the site. And some destructions are not due to a military onslaught, but may be the result of natural disasters.

modern Amman. The prominent mound was extensively excavated by devout Seventh Day Adventist archaeologists from 1968–1978, who no doubt confidently expected to find destruction levels dating to the late thirteenth century BCE or so. But the site was not really occupied before the twelfth to eleventh centuries BCE, and even then it was only a small, unfortified village—hardly the capital of Sihon, king of the Amorites (Num. 21:34). The excavators, excellent archaeologists, faced up to the problem gallantly, and they declared Heshbon to be "the first casualty in the war," that is, in their own battle to confirm Scripture.

The site of Dibon has fared no better. Again, the location is not in doubt—biblical Dibon is the mound of *Dhiban* in Arabic, farther south in Moab. It was excavated in the 1950s and 1960s, again by conservative American Christian scholars, this time Southern Baptists. Here there seem to be no remains whatsoever before the ninth century BCE. This is indeed miraculous—a city that was not even there was conquered!

But there is more. Pressing northward, the Hebrew forces turned to the east bank of the Jordan river, opposite Jericho. The imposing site of ancient Jericho—the largest *tell* in the lower Jordan valley—has been excavated several times in the twentieth century, notably by the legendary British archaeologist Dame Kathleen Kenyon in 1952–1958.

It is clear that the site had been destroyed ca. 1500 BCE by the Egyptians, then virtually deserted until a small Israelite town was founded in the seventh century BCE. Again, there was no Canaanite city to have been destroyed, no walls to come tumbling down.

It would seem that the biblical writers in the seventh century BCE knew of the Israelite village at Jericho. They might even have seen the stubs of the old ruined mudbrick city walls from the destruction centuries earlier, some still visible today. But there is no Israelite destruction. Nor can biblical Jericho be located anywhere else in the lower Jordan valley; there are no other mounds anywhere nearby.

The next obvious target coming up from Jericho to the central hill country was the site of 'Ai—the "ruin heap" discussed above. The complex biblical story of its supposed destruction is told in Joshua 6–7. Here, too, the location of biblical 'Ai is not in dispute. Excavations of the great twenty-seven-acre mound were carried out by French excavators in 1933–1935, and again by American excavators in 1964–1970, the latter directed by Southern Baptist scholar Joseph Calloway. Here the silence of the text is deafening: there are no remains. The site was entirely abandoned by about 2500 BCE and remained deserted until a small Israelite village was founded directly on those ruins, probably in the twelfth century BCE.

There is no Israelite destruction because there is not so much as a Late Bronze Age Canaanite potsherd on the entire site. The excavator, Joseph Calloway, a southern gentleman, took early retirement from his professorship at the Southern Baptist seminary in Louisville, having failed to confirm Joshua's famed conquest of the site.

A few other scholars (mostly fundamentalists) tried another tactic to "save" (destroy?) 'Ai. They insisted that the story of destruction was really about Canaanite Bethel, only about two miles distant, which does have a destruction level dating to ca. 1200 BCE. The story got displaced to Bethel by mistake, since 'Ai—"the ruin heap," as its name means—must have been so obvious that some site got destroyed. Other scholars attempt to locate biblical 'Ai somewhere else, which is unlikely since "the ruin" is obviously the mound discussed here, still prominent today.

The rest of the book of Joshua is devoted to a series of military campaigns, first in the central hills, then in the Hebron hills to the south, and finally in Galilee to the north. These campaigns evidently covered no more than a few months. There is no need to summarize the accounts here in the light of archaeological evidence. The story is simple and stark.

Of all the total thirty-eight sites that Joshua (and Numbers) claims were "utterly destroyed," there is really only one candidate for any destruction in the light of what we now know: Hazor, "the head of all those kingdoms." The account of the fiery destruction and the annihilation of the entire populace is contained in Joshua 11. The site was extensively excavated by the famed Israeli archaeologist Yigael Yadin in 1955–1958, and again by Amnon Ben-Tor in 1990–2017.

Here there really *is* a destruction—and a horrific one. The Canaanite palace-temple complex is burnt to the ground sometime in the late thirteenth century BCE. Statues are beheaded; cultic and other vessels are smashed to pieces. The site is so badly damaged that it lies in ruins, deserted for more than a century. It looks like more than destruction; someone is taking it out on the inhabitants. But who?

According to Joshua 11:10–14, the Israelites unleashed their fury on Hazor, not only because it was the mightiest city in Canaan, but principally because Yahweh had directly commanded it. Joshua "left nothing undone of all that Yahweh had commanded Moses" (Josh. 11:15). Yadin had confidently identified Joshua's Israelites as the destroyers. Ben-Tor generally agrees, but he is not quite as dogmatic. His co-director, the late Sharon Zuckerman, thinks that internecine war between rival Canaanite rulers is a more likely explanation. There the matter rests. But out of the thirty-eight cities said to be destroyed, that is not very good odds.

Elsewhere in Canaan we do find some destructions on this horizon. But they are mostly along the coast, where the Philistines are known to have been invading from Cyprus and the Aegean world in precisely this period. A few others may be due to natural disasters. A number of major Canaanite sites, like Megiddo and Gezer, are not destroyed or even disturbed at all; they continue unabated until ca. 1000 BCE. So there is no total Canaanite destruction.

According to our scenario, only a very few sites—perhaps only one—can be related with some confidence to Israelite destructions under Joshua. Some conservative biblical scholars try to get around this dilemma by arguing that the Bible does not *really* claim the wholesale destruction of Canaanite sites. Only three are said to have been "burned": Jericho, 'Ai, and Hazor. Indeed, Joshua 11:13 states that most of the relevant sites were not burned, only Hazor (ignoring the contradiction).

Nevertheless, the biblical stories are consistent in claiming that *all* the sites were "destroyed" (except Gibeon and Shechem, taken in by covenant). Can one really assume that the Canaanite inhabitants conveniently fled, so that there was no need for armed conflict? What clearly happened was (or would have been) genocide; and it was Yahweh's will. Believers and nonbelievers will have to deal with that one way or another. The biblical story, overall, cannot be "saved."

In addition to Hazor, Bethel may also witness an Israelite destruction (cf. above). But all that we know for certain is that there appears to be a small Israelite village of the twelfth century BCE above the ruins. Tel Zayit, a small mound on the Philistine border in Judah, is also destroyed ca. 1200 BCE, but apparently by the Philistines. It may be identified as biblical Libnah, the destruction of which Joshua 10:29–30 attributes to the Israelites, but that seems less likely.

The mention again of Hazor, which is claimed to have been completely destroyed by Joshua in chapter 11, brings us to another bit of conflicting data. In the Hebrew Bible there is a second account of the rise of early Israel in the book of Judges, put by the original editors back-to-back with the book of Joshua. And it is very different. In chapters 1–4 we find the famous list of Canaanite sites said *not* to have been taken. Among them, somewhat surprisingly, is Hazor, whose King Jabin is said to be still functioning, not dead at all (Judg. 4:17; compare Josh. 11:11–12). Not only that, he is said to have had nine hundred chariots (Judg. 4:2, 3). He is killed (again!) only later in Judges 4:24.

Furthermore, the whole book of Judges is the epochal story of some twelve consecutive charismatic tribal leaders, raised up by Yahweh over several generations, covering as many as two hundred years. They are not primarily "judges," but military leaders. Their specific challenge is to lead the Israelite tribes to victory against the Canaanites, who are specifically said to be still living in the land.

One of these warriors is a woman, Deborah. Her victory against the Canaanite king Sisera, aided by another woman, Yael, who actually kills him, is celebrated in one of the oldest poems preserved in the Hebrew Bible, the "Song of Deborah" (Judg. 5), which may date to the twelfth century BCE.

To sum up, the biblical writers and editors gave us two, almost diametrically opposed accounts of their own origins. Why? It may be that they had different sources, although both books belong to the same date, that of the Deuteronomistic historians working in the seventh century BCE. On the other hand, they may have been more sophisticated than we think they were. They knew that the settlement process that had begun centuries ago in Canaan was indeed an exceedingly complicated process. Did they include two versions, fully realizing how different they were, just to be honest historians? Or did they want to force us to think more critically about the matter?

In any case, we must be grateful for the authors' candor. But for the archaeologist, in command of data that they didn't have, the account in Judges has "the ring of truth" about it and may be earlier (as we shall see in the next chapter). In contrast, Joshua is almost certainly a work of fiction, celebrating in an exaggerated fashion the exploits of a legendary military hero.

To sum up, our archaeological critique of the biblical exodus and conquest stories may seem quite negative. It certainly makes a simplistic reading of the biblical text rather difficult. Yet that may be how it is supposed to be. As we have seen, there are two contrasting versions of what happened in the Bible itself. The book of Joshua tells the story of a lightning-fast military conquest of all of Canaan under the command of one man, Joshua. After that, the land simply becomes a new entity, "Israel."

The book of Judges, however, tells a very different story. Here the Canaanites are not vanquished at all. That will take another two hundred years of
more gradual social, economic, and cultural change—a process of evolution,
even religious revolution. What happened, then, was not a military clash at
all, except perhaps for a few early skirmishes. The *real* battle came later. It was
a clash of ideas, which was won only slowly and painfully. It was a very long
time before Yahwism would prevail. Perhaps "God works in mysterious ways,
his wonders to perform," as the old Scottish hymn has it.

But so far, we have gotten the Israelites only to the border of the promised
land. The subsequent settlement process will be equally problematic; and here,
archaeology will be not only our primary source, but virtually our only source
(see below, Chapter 4).

What Is Left and Does It Matter?

In this chapter we have taken a revisionist approach to the books of Exodus,
Numbers, and Joshua with their narratives of the miraculous exodus of the
Hebrews from Egypt and a whirlwind conquest of all Canaan. We have been
more positive about the relatively modest account in the book of Judges. But
either way, our reconstruction of this formative era of Israelite history requires
a reinterpretation of the biblical text in the specific light of the archaeological
data. So what have we learned?

The subplot of the book of Exodus is first that the evil Pharaoh will not
prevail forever; he will be toppled when enough people revolt. And if they are
still a minority, they may yet succeed, not by military might, but by superior
moral authority—given a leader adequate for the hour. The underdog *can*
win. And that victory will always seem miraculous, because it defies human
imagination.

Second, the journey to any promised land is perilous. There are innumerable false starts, detours, and sidetracks. Some will lose sight of the distant
goal, rebel, and foolishly want to turn back. Some may die. However optimistic
we are at the outset, many will despair, and some will be lost, even perhaps a
whole generation. The road inevitably leads through the wilderness; but the
hardships there forge *character*, without which all is lost. But one survives, and
that is what counts in human terms. Ideals persist despite all the odds, above
all the ideal of freedom. Even if the ideal is never fulfilled, there are oases in
the desert, and the wilderness eventually does end. In any case, the journey
may be more significant than the destination. We are all pilgrims.

These are difficult lessons from Exodus, Numbers, and Judges, but those to be learned from the book of Joshua are indeed painful. There the narrative is all about holy war, commanded by an angry, vengeful, and violent Yahweh, whose blood lust is quenched by nothing less than the extermination of all his enemies. He uses human agents to accomplish his aims, even if they themselves are demonized in the process. The end justifies the means. This message must be rejected by any sensitive and decent person. It is wrong. Sometimes the Bible teaches us by a negative lesson. Then there is the theme of unqualified obedience to the law. Those who break the law, willfully or innocently, will be punished; there is no forgiveness.

Yet there are a few more humane notions in Joshua. The whole land of Canaan is not subdued by violence, because violence doesn't always prevail. Some of the land remains; and all of it is finally a gift, not the result of seizure. And the work of redemption is always unfinished; Joshua dies before it is accomplished. There are no simple solutions. As the old proverb has it: "Man proposes; God disposes." The biblical writers knew that, and so did the early Greek philosophers who had almost the same expression.

Now we come at last to the book of Judges with a sigh of relief. The stories here are more accessible, more human, and more believable. They are not so much about miracles as they are about real life. Here we see writ large an incredibly diverse society: Canaanites; Egyptians; Israelites; Philistines; Arameans; all the varied peoples of Transjordan; and those other "-ites"—the Amalekites, Hivites, Midianites, Perizzites, and other mysterious folk.

We now know that this was the actual society of Canaan in the Iron I era in the wake of the collapse of the more homogenous Bronze Age societies in the Levant in the thirteenth century BCE. The end came not in sudden, sweeping destructions, but in a protracted, painful process of collapse, as one subsystem after another failed. Gradually new peoples coalesced again, and new societies gained a foothold. Nevertheless, continuing cultural clashes were inevitable. Change is slow.

The colorful stories in Judges are told against the backdrop of this Iron I world. The successive "judges" are heroic individuals who rise up, one after another, to meet the social challenges using a combination of folk wisdom, cunning, populist sentiments, even deceit, but always with a pragmatic acceptance of the limits of their own abilities.

These are profoundly human characters. Gideon is a strapping farm lad, intent upon plowing his fields, suspicious of "angels," and not ready for any mission. Jephthah is a fool, whose hasty vow costs him his beloved daughter's life. Deborah, a woman in a man's world, dares to sit in judgment under a tree in the countryside; she has no courtroom. Samson, the greatest hero of them all, dies ignominiously because he was fascinated by the wrong woman. But these quite ordinary people somehow had quite extraordinary gifts—yes, gifts. And they made a difference. One individual can make a difference, but not without a little help.

In the end, however, no matter how we humanize the Bible's larger-than-life stories about an exodus and conquest of Canaan, one nagging question remains. In the great biblical epic of Israel's history, from the beginning of the world to the fall of Jerusalem and the hope of an eventual messiah, the dramatic story of the exodus from Egypt and the conquest of the promised land is the *focal point*. Everything hinges on these pivotal events. But if these things didn't actually happen this way, how did such a story ever get into the Hebrew Bible? More to the point, how could it have become the basis of Israel's existence and its enduring faith, even to this day?

The question is complex but fair, and there may be a relatively simple answer. We need to remember that the biblical story was composed and edited in the south, in the kingdom of Judah, and it reflects that perspective. It is significant that some elements of the biblical story, like the long Joseph cycle (Gen. 37–50), seem to show that the central tribes that border Judah are the tribes of Ephraim and Manasseh, that is, those who were thought to have been direct descendants of Joseph. And these two tribes, with Benjamin, are sometimes referred to in the Hebrew Bible as "the House of Joseph." This scenario suggests that the biblical story, as it stands, is really the story of two or three small central and southern tribes, some of whose members may really have been slaves escaping from Egypt. And in retrospect, it all really did seem miraculous to them— miraculous that they survived at all. As their story was told again and again, it quite naturally expanded to include "all Israel," as in the final biblical version. Yet the fact is that most of the ancient Israelites had never been in Egypt. They were displaced Canaanites—displaced both geographically and culturally. Yet it became their story, too. So, there *was* an "exodus group" after all—just not one quite so miraculous. It may have comprised only a few hundred people.

This is not simply an imaginative reading, one divorced from a biblical reality. The Passover *Haggadah* has included almost from the beginning a libretto to the dramatic reenactment of the exodus, in which is declared: "It is as though *we* had been in Egypt, and have been delivered by the Almighty to this very day." But literally speaking, "we" were never in Egypt, Jews or others today. Yet we resonate with the Passover story because it is a story of the *liberation* for which we all long, and can find in community, in common memories.

There is also an instructive parallel in American history. On Thanksgiving Day, we all celebrate our Pilgrim origins as though we *all* had come over on the Mayflower. But most of us are not even distant descendants of the Pilgrim Fathers. We have entirely different origins, more so than ever in our pluralistic, multicultural, multiethnic society. Yet on Thanksgiving Day, we are all *Americans*. And it is our common ideological origin, our shared ethnic self-identity, that makes us Americans. The metaphor *is* the reality.

CHAPTER 4

Israel Settles in Its Land of Promise—or Peril?

Prologue

The book of Judges follows Joshua in the Hebrew Bible thematically and chronologically. It takes up the story after Joshua's death, where things end with the Israelites on the ground in Canaan, though not yet settled. As we shall see, Judges now charts a much longer and more complex course of socioeconomic and cultural development as an identifiable "early Israel" emerges in Canaan *vis-à-vis* the collapsing Canaanite culture, now in its dying gasp. It was a long, drawn-out process of ethnogenesis, in which Israel gradually distinguished itself from Canaanite culture between ca. 1200 and 1000 BCE when the Israelite state arises. This would correspond with the biblical "period of the Judges," described in some detail in the book by that name. In essence, Iron Age Israel replaces Late Bronze Age Canaan as the latter is collapsing. But what environmental, cultural, and political factors *caused* such a collapse?

The long Bronze Age or "Canaanite" culture in the Levant (ancient Syria-Palestine) lasted with remarkable persistence and continuity from the mid-fourth millennium BCE until the mid- to late thirteenth century BCE, when things literally fell apart. The disaster was not confined, however, to the Levant.

All within a century or less, the palace civilizations of Greece and the Aegean world eclipsed, the Hittite kingdom in Anatolia (modern Turkey) totally ceased to exist, the New Kingdom in Egypt degenerated into the Third Intermediate Period, and the Middle Assyrian and Kassite empires in Mesopotamia fell into decline. The Late Bronze Age gave way to the Iron Age. What went so drastically wrong?

Scholars have wrestled with the perennial question of empire collapse for decades. What caused the fall of the Roman empire? All civilizations and cultures come to an end. Attempting to explain these phenomena, one thing is clear: there are no simple explanations, because there is never a single cause. There are many complex, interacting factors in any society's eventual demise.

In the case of the end of the Late Bronze Age in the Mediterranean world and beyond, various causative factors have been suggested. These include political factors, such as the overthrow of autocratic regimes (that is, popular uprisings) or invasions by foreign peoples. There may also have been socioeconomic factors, such as class warfare. The advent of new ideologies, especially religious ones, can usher in an era of profound and even radical upheaval. Population growth can get beyond control and, like other changes, can force large-scale relocations of peoples, creating a sort of domino effect. Then there are natural disasters, such as prolonged droughts, exhaustion of environmental resources, earthquakes, floods, tsunamis, and the like.

The point is that no single one of these factors is likely to have been sufficient to cause a sudden or widespread calamity, but a combination of one or more factors may trigger a chain reaction that will eventually result in a total collapse. It is the notion of "collapse" that dominates the discussion today. The analogy is borrowed from the natural sciences, assuming that human societies can be expected to behave similarly. In any living organism, life is a system that is sustained by the intricate interaction of a number of subsystems. Thus human health and well-being depend upon the simultaneous coordination of the respiratory, cardiac, vascular, alimentary, reproductive, sensory, and cognitive subsystems. If one fails, the body may survive; but further degeneration ensues in a systemic failure, eventually resulting in a total collapse. Death inevitably results.

The analogy of social systems collapsing like biological systems is often called "General Systems Theory," and it has been effectively employed in archaeology. Here the most pertinent social subsystems are settlement type and distribution; demographic change; socioeconomic structures; political organization; technology; broader culture phenomena such as literacy, art, aesthetics, and religion; and finally external contacts.

The archaeologist works essentially with culture and cultural change; and "culture" is patterned adaptation. A culture adapts or it dies, and adaptation is always multifaceted. The key concept here is "equilibrium"—the delicate maintenance of a balance between all the cultural subsystems. If one subsystem fails it can trigger a sort of downward spiral that leads to other failures, until the whole system spins out of control. The result is systemic collapse. That is what

Culture

"Culture" refers to a pattern of collective socioeconomic, political, and aesthetic adaptation to a particular environment, both physical and psychological. That is how our species, like all species, survives: we adapt or perish.

Archaeologists are particularly concerned with "material culture," which refers specifically to the phenomenon of culture as defined by successive phases of artifactual evidence (as opposed to textual evidence). Archaeology depends on its ability to describe a particular culture—like that of ancient Israel—by characterizing artifacts as "material correlates" that embody cultural patterns and give them meaning. Thus we can make larger inferences, or educated guesses, about what it was like in the remote past.

This does not result in a perfect history—there is none—but it provides us with a reasonable portrait.

apparently happened at the end of the Levantine Bronze Age. There were indeed widespread disruptions, invasions, and relocations of several ethnic groups (including the Israelites). But that was the result of the crisis, not its cause.

There were several earthquakes known on this horizon, and at one time that led some scholars to attribute all the cultural upheavals to this factor. Technological change has also been invoked. A few scholars thought that the invention of superior iron weapons triggered the advent of the Iron Age; that is, warfare was the engine of change. (This idea was popularized in Jared Diamond's *Guns, Germs, and Steel*, though not specifically in relation to the Iron Age Levant.)

It has been proposed that a prolonged, widespread drought was the ultimate factor, but the environmental data are scant and difficult to quantify. In any case, no one can doubt that the result was catastrophic. In the "cradle of civilization" in the Mediterranean world, it seemed like the infant had died. Civilization had come to an end.

But it was not the end. Catastrophe is always followed by what we may call "anastrophe," a building up again. The evolutionary process of civilization is a cycle of rise and fall and rise again. Part of this process is now seen to be the fact that "equilibrium" is an abstract and possibly misleading idea. It appears that most civilizations are not really stable at all. The appearance of stability is the result of a fragile and ephemeral balance, one that is readily tipped by any number of variables. Ironically, the meddling of reformers and social engineers can sometimes make matters worse. Collapse may simply be inevitable. No civilization is immortal, because humans are not.

Early Israel first appears in the light of history precisely in the Dark Age following the twilight at the end of the Canaanite Late Bronze Age, ca. 1350–1250

BCE. To understand how that unlikely event may have happened, we need to see it as a process, one that occurred in a particular context.

The Egyptian New Kingdom (Dynasties 18–20) had annexed Canaan and ruled it with an iron hand for nearly three hundred years. Its rapacious rule is vividly portrayed in an archive of cuneiform tablets found in Egypt in the late nineteenth century, known as the "Amarna tablets" from their findspot, Tell el-Amarna, the capital of the Egyptian pharaoh Ahkenaten. These are letters sent in part to the court of the famous pharaoh, known as the "heretic king" for his peculiarities, including introducing a form of monotheism. However, he seems to have been too busy with that and his beautiful Queen Nefertiti to have answered his mail, so we don't have the other end of the correspondence.

The letters contain mostly gossip and compliments sent to the pharaoh from rival Canaanite petty princes vying for favors. They malign one another and offer tribute in the form of gold and silver, precious stones, linen garments, and even concubines and slaves. One letter from Labayu, the king of Shechem, mentions a rebellious, outcast group known as the *Apiru* (it sounds cognate with "Hebrew," but it is not). He declares:

> Further, the king wrote concerning my son. I did not know that my son associates with the Apiru, and I have verily delivered him into the hand of Adday (the local Egyptian high commissioner). Further, if the king should write for my wife, how could I withhold her? If the king should write to me "Plunge a bronze dagger into thy heart and die!" how could I refuse to carry out the command of the king?[1]

In another letter, the king of Megiddo requests a troop of only a hundred Egyptian warriors to go against his rival Labayu of Shechem, showing how petty the struggles were.

All in all, the Amarna letters demonstrate how Late Bronze Age Canaan was divided, badly managed, and impoverished by the fourteenth to thirteenth centuries BCE. The decline would accelerate, and by the twelfth century the successors of the great Ramesses II had retreated to a few desolate Egyptian forts in Canaan. By 1150 BCE or so, they abandoned the last outposts altogether, in part threatened by invasions in southern Canaan by a new group of invaders known as the "Sea Peoples."

The Sea Peoples consisted of various groups of displaced peoples, principally of Mycenaean Greek heritage, who migrated into the Aegean islands,

---

1. El-Amarna letter 254, lines 30–46.

then settled briefly on Cyprus before invading the coast of Canaan ca. 1185 BCE. The invasions of the Sea Peoples are known from pictorial reliefs as well as inscriptions from the time of Ramesses III showing their attempted invasion of the Nile delta by both land and sea. The texts date to the fifth and eighth year of Ramesses III. One reads:

> The foreign lands made a conspiracy in their islands. Agitated and scattered in battle were the lands at one time. . . . Their league comprised the Philis-tines (*peleset*), Sicels, Shakalusha, Danuna, and Washash.

Ramesses III later claimed to have expanded the borders of Egypt, slaughtering the Philistines and other "Sea Peoples" and settling the survivors in forts.

There are other Sea Peoples in this and other inscriptions, but one group, the *peleset,* are clearly the biblical "Philistines." They appear on the coast of Canaan just a generation or so after the earliest Israelite settlements in the hill country— another element of the cultural mix in the Iron I period. The later biblical writ-ers are acquainted with Philistines as contemporaries and rivals. The Israelites avoid them in Joshua's attempted invasion, making an end run into Transjordan and then into Canaan by the back door via Jericho. Later they are described as (1) newcomers from Caphtor (Crete) in the Aegean world; (2) uncircumcised (that is, non-Semitic); (3) organized into a five-city league comprising Ashkelon, Ashdod, Gath, Ekron, and Gaza along the southern coast; and (4) expanding inland to threaten the Israelite settlement in the period of the judges.

This may be scant information, but recent archaeological excavations of all but one of the pentapolis sites (Gaza) have illuminated Philistine culture even more brilliantly than that of the early Israelites. All of the somewhat cryptic information concerning the Philistines in the Hebrew Bible has proven correct, even though they are portrayed as "the bad guys" and are hardly the focus of the stories. Their material culture is easily recognizable on the basis of archaeological remains. They include distinctive painted pottery (some im-ported from Cyprus); the urban layout of sites; "megaron" buildings; hearths; superior weapons; exotic art and cultic paraphernalia; unique burial customs; foreign deities; and a hitherto undeciphered script that seems to resemble Linear A or B.

There are other players on the stage by the twelfth century BCE as well. The Phoenicians along the northern coast (near modern Haifa) had inherited the language and customs of the collapsing Canaanite culture. Phoenician sites like Acco and Dor are mentioned in Judges. Farther north in Syria, the Aramean city-states, which will soon rival Israel, were arising. In Transjordan,

Philistines

The ancient people known as Philistines were characterized mostly on the basis of the Hebrew Bible until the late nineteenth century. The first archaeological evidence was the discovery of elaborate bichrome pottery found in Palestine that looked very similar to Late Bronze Age Mycenaean wares. This possible ethnic clue was then linked to several Egyptian texts already known at the time, especially texts found on the walls of the mortuary temple of Ramesses III at Karnak (1184–1153 BCE).

These Egyptian texts, dated to Ramesses's fifth and eighth years, describe and also illustrate in paintings the invasion of the Nile delta by land and sea by a group described as "Sea Peoples." Among the peoples named in this group are the *peleset*, certainly our biblical "Philistines."

Despite the Philistines being the archenemies of nascent Israel, the biblical writers describe them with some accuracy. And today we have so much supplementary data from archaeology that we could write a history of the Philistines as comprehensive as that of early Israel.

the petty kingdoms of Ammon, Moab, and Edom—all closely related to Israel in language and culture—were slowly emerging. Thus, the vacuum created by the collapse of the Late Bronze Age Canaan was being filled by new peoples, among them the "Proto-Israelites" (see further below).

The Biblical Narrative

The book of Judges is all we have in the Bible to cover nearly two hundred years of early Israel's history. But it does not really describe any of the numerous early Israelite settlements that we actually know from their archaeological remains; it only names a few in passing. That is not because the writers, giving their account several centuries later, had no information. The reason is rather that, like all ancient historians, their instinct was to tell stories—not simply to chronicle events (real or imaginary), but more importantly to drive home a lesson or moral point. In short, history teaches us how to behave, what the gods require.

The numerous stories in Judges revolve around a series of a dozen or more successive judges (thus the name) and their experiences. They were charismatic individuals, raised up by Yahweh to rally the tribes and deal with the challenges of a multicultural society in turmoil. Contrary to the idealistic scenario in the book of Joshua, the Israelites had not inherited their promised land—far from it. Although these officials are called "judges" (Hebrew *shofet)*, administering justice was not their primary role. Their real role was to provide *ad hoc* leadership, specifically as Yahweh's champions in holy war (another form of justice). They had a vocation, literally a "calling."

The judges, many of whom were minor figures, did not necessarily serve consecutively. The stock formula may say "and *x* judged Israel for *y* years," but many of these individuals probably overlapped, some of them being only regional representatives out of the mainstream.

By the best calculations, the combined careers of the judges covered about 160 years. That would extend from ca. 1180 BCE, early in the settlement era in the Iron I period, to the inauguration of the first king, Saul, ca. 1020 BCE. This was a formative, pre-state period. "In those days there was no king in Israel, and every man did what was right in his own eyes" (Judg. 17:6). Space precludes recounting all their stories. We will only highlight what can be learned from three of their stories: those of Gideon, Deborah, and Samson.

Samson is a failed hero (Judg. 13–16). An angel tells his mother that he will deliver the Israelites from their mortal enemy, the Philistines. He becomes a "Nazirite," an ascetic devotee of Yahweh, so Yahweh's spirit descends upon him. But he compromises his vows, and his unquenchable lust betrays him. He does perform a few miracles, and he kills a few Philistines. But he is entranced by Delilah, and she tricks him. In the process of trying to take revenge against Yahweh's enemies, the ungodly Philistines, Samson becomes their prisoner. He dies defiantly at Ashkelon, bringing their pagan Temple of Dagon down around his and their heads. Not much of a deliverance. Is this a true story? And can we learn anything from it?

There are, of course, genuine historical details that emerge, many of them congruent with the archaeological data that we now have. The Philistines really were contemporaries of early Israel, they were arrayed along the borders of Judah, and they did constitute an existential threat. The description of their wheat fields, vineyards, and orchards does indeed reflect an ethnic group who were not merely invaders but were, by now, well established settlers. The deity Dagon at Ashkelon is well known as a Canaanite deity, so the Philistines were by now partly acculturated. The references to weaving are corroborated by archaeological evidence that shows weaving to have been an "ethnic trait" of the Philistines. Timnah (Tel Batash) has been extensively excavated, and it has produced all the ethnic markers that distinguish it from nearby Israelite sites, like Beth-Shemesh.

The most important aspect of the Samson epic, however, is how realistically it portrays an open, porous border typical of a multiethnic society. Samson lives at the camp of Dan, and in the evenings he strolls down the nearby Sorek Valley to visit Delilah. He is an Israelite, she a Philistine; but there is no border control, no passports required. Nevertheless, their liaison is forbidden, and in the end it proves disastrous.

The lesson is that you must not fraternize with the enemy. It is a betrayal of your people and your own self-identity, and it will be punished. Make no mistake, this story is not about infidelity (Samson is married); it is about a more serious betrayal, betrayal of Yahweh, Israel's husband.

Another morality play is the story of Gideon (Judg. 6–9). The backdrop is that the Midianites, a people from southern Transjordan, and the Amalekites (unknown) have arisen against the Israelite tribes. An angel appears to Gideon under an oak tree (trees being associated with shrines).

Gideon has been threshing wheat near a winepress in his father's fields. He now brashly complains to the angel about harsh conditions and asks why Yahweh has forsaken the Israelites. The angel commands Gideon to "save Israel," but Gideon protests that he is a poor, obscure man, "the least in his father's house" (Judg. 6:15). The angel promises to help and offers as a sign the acceptance of a food offering. So Gideon prepares a sacrifice, lays it on a rock altar, sees it magically lit afire, and accepts his calling.

That night Gideon assembles ten men from his father's house (the typical Israelite multigenerational patrimonial household) for fear of reprisals. He then sends messengers to rally all the men of the tribes of Manasseh, Zebulun, and Naphtali. Winnowing down the volunteers to three hundred men, and adding other tribal forces, Gideon attacks and vanquishes all Yahweh's enemies.

In due time, Gideon (now renamed "Jerubbaal," a pagan name) proceeds to the old tribal center at Shechem, where Abraham had first visited the shrine. There he is acclaimed as a ruler; but he modestly declines, declaring "Yahweh shall rule over you." But then Gideon makes a forbidden ephod (an adornment made only by and for priests) and installs it in his home village, where "all Israel goes a-whoring after it" (Judg. 8:27). Apostasy or not, Israel is said to have been at peace for the next forty years.

Our final story is about a woman, Deborah (Judg. 4–5). Deborah would be remarkable by any standards, especially in Israel where men ruled unchallenged. She is actually a functioning judge, although she has no tribunal, and she renders verdicts that are presumably binding. She is also a prophetess (*nebi'ah*), which means that she is a spokesperson for Yahweh. The story has to do with how Jabin, king of Hazor (said to have been killed in the book of Joshua) threatens to oppress the Israelites with a force of nine hundred chariots. Deborah recruits ten thousand men, and with the general Barak she attacks Jabin, wrecks his chariots, and slaughters the entire lot. With the help of another heroic woman, Yael, Jabin's general Sisera is lured into a tent, made drunk, and killed by a tent peg driven into his temple. All this is celebrated as the work of Yahweh.

Despite the enduring fascination of these and other memorable stories in the book of Judges, we learn almost nothing about the Israelite settlements on the ground. A number of sites (approximately twenty) are mentioned, however, as settings for the stories, and most of them can now be identified. At least half of them have been excavated, and indeed, most do exhibit Israelite ethnic markers. On the other hand, more than a dozen sites are mentioned in Judges as being non-Israelite, and, perhaps surprisingly, nearly all of them can now be shown on the basis of the current archaeological evidence to be ethnically Canaanite, Philistine, or Phoenician.

Despite their artlessness, the biblical writers had surprisingly accurate, detailed information about early Israelite sites, even though they were writing centuries later. Here the book of Judges seems to incorporate many older, more authentic sources than Joshua, even though it too has an obvious theological bias. But their stories tell us all that the authors were interested in: Israel's faithlessness compromises the great conquest of Canaan under Joshua. Foreign oppressors continue to threaten the social and religious solidarity of the community. Even heroes blessed by Yahweh's spirit cannot save the people if they have no power. A king may be the only remedy. So Samuel—the last of the judges and the first effective prophet—was beseeched to appoint a king for the Israelites like the Canaanites had. That act will see the transition from informal charismatic leadership to institutionalized kingship. But it will also represent progress. The book of Judges ends with the familiar refrain "In those days there was no king in Israel; all the people did what was right in their own eyes" (Judg. 21:25; cf. 17:6). Now a king will bring order.

Having learned so far little of the facts on the ground concerning early Israel, let us probe a bit deeper before turning to modern archaeological data. With insights gained from the latter, we see that there is more than meets the eye in the laconic biblical narratives in the book of Judges.

If we attempt to extrapolate from the textual data, taking specific references from the book of Judges, the following picture emerges: (1) Early Israel consists of a number of small, rural villages, isolated from the continuing Canaanite towns like Megiddo and Gezer, and even more so from newly established Philistine cities such as Ashkelon. These villages do not seem to supplant ruined Canaanite towns, but represent new foundations. There are few Israelite sites in the north, like Dan. There are more sites in the central hill country: Bethel,

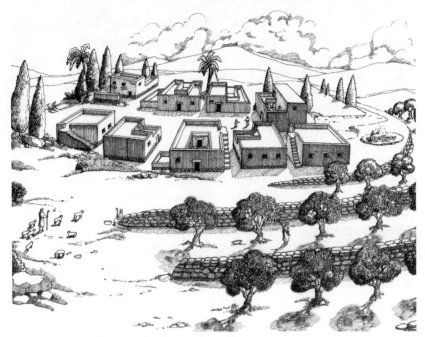

Reconstruction of a typical early Israelite village

Gibeah, Mizpah, and Shiloh. In the southern hills of Judah, Hebron and Arad are mentioned.

(2) The agrarian economy and society are based on a pattern of kin-related, egalitarian extended families or clans. A patrimonial system assigns rural lands to these groups and secures their inheritance. The individual family household is the base of the society.

(3) There is no centralized form of government. There are only local shrines (and deities). The clans are semiautonomous and often at odds with one another, especially over clan allotments. They are rallied and united briefly only by occasional folk heroes to engage the Philistines and other non-Israelite people in the land. But the borders remain open and subject to change by either negotiation or force. This is a decentralized, multiethnic, and multicultural world, one in flux.

As time goes on (into the eleventh century BCE) the situation grows worse, not better. Clan relations are inherently unstable and the militias are small, disorganized, and poorly armed. According to 1 Samuel 13:19–22, the Philistines have a monopoly on weapons. The situation grows so dire that Israel, scarcely born, seems about to expire.

All this is a far cry from Joshua's "finished conquest" by a covenantally united community. The later orthodox writers and editors of the book of Judges acknowledge the crisis. But they blame it on the incompetence of the judges, and even more so on the rebellious Israelite peasants, who do not deserve Yahweh's promise of bounty. "The Israelites did what was evil in the sight of Yahweh" (Judg. 3:7). The final section of the book chronicles Israel's gradual demise (Judg. 17–21).

The story in Judges is gripping. The places and peoples seem real enough, but are any of the larger-than-life judges real historical persons? Archaeology corroborates the general context of Judges and fills in numerous lacunae dramatically, as we shall see. While there are many details that we shall never be able to substantiate, especially those of individual lives, we can say that there is *nothing* of the general situation of early Israel and its socioeconomic context in the twelfth to eleventh centuries BCE, so vividly portrayed in the book of Judges, that does not fit well into the more fully fleshed-out picture obtained by recent archaeological evidence. To that evidence we now turn, seeing how it compares with both the books of Joshua and Judges.

An Archaeological Critique

The copious archaeological data, relevant as they are, are not any more self-explanatory than textual data. Both require interpretation to become meaningful. And a "model"—a working hypothesis—offers the best strategy. In the case of archaeology and early Israel, three models competed as the data mounted beginning in the 1930s. The first and more traditional model was, of course, derived from an uncritical reading of the exodus and conquest accounts in the biblical books of Exodus, Numbers, and Joshua. That model was already becoming obsolete by about 1960, when an American biblical scholar named George Mendenhall dared to suggest that there had been "no statistically significant" invasion of Canaan. That view has long since been fully confirmed by the archaeological data, as we have seen. Mendenhall went on, however, to declare:

> What happened instead may be termed, from the point of view of the secular historian interested only in socio-political processes, a peasants' revolt against the interlocking Canaanite city-states.[2]

2. George E. Mendenhall, "The Hebrew Conquest of Palestine," *Biblical Archaeologist* 25 (1962): 73.

Mendenhall was in many ways a maverick, but he was right—brilliantly right, since there was virtually no archaeological evidence to support his declaration at the time. We will return to his idea of revolting peasants shortly.

Already in the 1920s and 1930s, German scholars had put forward a model that might be called "peaceful infiltration." This model also rejected the biblical idea of a military conquest, and it focused instead on other biblical motifs. Abraham, Isaac, and Jacob, along with their extended families, are clearly portrayed in Genesis as pastoral nomads. They are tent-dwellers and sheepherders who migrate over long distances, very much like modern bedouin in the Middle East. This ethnographic analogy argued that the early Israelites had been pastoralists who came from Transjordan (as in the book of Numbers) and slowly and peacefully became fully sedentary in western Canaan across the Jordan. But there was then and now no archaeological evidence of such transhumants—not surprising, since migratory people seldom leave archaeological traces. From what we now know, nomads almost never settle willingly, since they prefer the desert lifestyle. Bedouin will insist that they are the *bedu,* the only *true* "Arabs of the Desert." They despise the *fellahin,* the petty farmers and merchants. To be sure, some of the early Israelites may have been pastoral nomads, like the Shasu bedouin discussed above, but probably only a minority.

The tribal language of the biblical narratives does not reflect an actual nomadic background as much as it does the kinship and clan structure of settled Israelite life in Canaan. It is a literary construct. Most earlier scholarly notions of a "tribal confederation" held together by a treaty, as in other known societies, have long since been given up.

The third model, derived from Mendenhall's "peasant revolt" theory, has proven to have more explanatory value, especially as more precise archaeological data have mounted. Even before the increase of archaeological corroboration, another prescient American scholar, Norman Gottwald, took the theory further in a Marxist scheme of "class warfare." This was elaborated in a bold 1979 work, the title of which is revealing: *The Tribes of Yahweh: A Sociology of the Religion of Liberated Israel, 1250–1050 BCE.* "Tribes," "Sociology," "Religion," "Liberated"—that says it all. But today that model as well is passé, except for one component: indigenous or local origins. That view, in one form or another, has won the day.

A variant is an "agrarian" or rural model put forward by some scholars. It also emphasizes indigenous origins, as well as a certain kind of socioeconomic revolution, but it sets aside the presumption that religion (in this case Yahwism) played a major role. Ideology certainly did, in the form embraced by many agrarian movements that adopt a goal of land reform, setting up egalitarianism and the "good life" of independent farmers as the ideal.

Yahwistic practices may have been present in early Israel here and there, but the widespread Yahwistic *monotheism* of the later biblical scenario is largely a late literary construct, the reality later still. In any case, we have only a few Iron I cult sites, and none that are specifically dedicated to an identifiable deity (see "Conclusion").

It may be helpful here to discuss not just the theories, but what we now actually know about early Israel. In summarizing the archaeological data it will be convenient to utilize the General Systems Theory introduced above, treating each subsystem in turn.

(1) *Settlement Patterns and Demography.* Changing settlement patterns are among our best archaeological clues to cultural change. The Late Bronze Age settlement pattern consists of a dozen or so relatively central cities, some with a population of up to twenty thousand. Each dominates a hinterland of smaller towns and villages in a multi-tiered hierarchical pattern of distribution. To be sure, these sites had mostly declined, and some had been deserted as a result of major upheavals in the thirteenth century BCE as the Canaanite culture tottered to an end.

During the Iron I period (ca. 1200–1000 BCE) there is a dramatic shift in settlement patterns. Some cities and towns continue, particularly Canaanite and Philistine sites. But in the central hill country there are several hundred new, dispersed, non-nucleated sites. They are hamlets or small villages, nearly all established *de novo* rather than on older or ruined Canaanite sites. Most of the sites were discovered in surface surveys, but a few have been excavated.

There is a reason for this shift. It is estimated that the combined Late Bronze population of the hill country was no more than about twelve thousand. But by the early Iron I era, it had swelled to some forty thousand, and by the eleventh century BCE it had grown to between fifty and sixty thousand. This population explosion is far too great to be explained by natural increase alone. There must have been a substantial influx of newcomers from elsewhere. The rapid highland settlement and growth is due to the fact that this area was a sparsely occupied frontier, attractive and open for colonization. We shall argue below that these settlers were displaced Canaanites, who became our early "Israelites."

(2) *Site Type and Distribution.* The numerous highland villages are all un-walled, often simply located on hilltops for defense. Their populations range from a few dozen up to a maximum of about three hundred. None have any real urban features, such as a planned layout or any type of monumental archi-

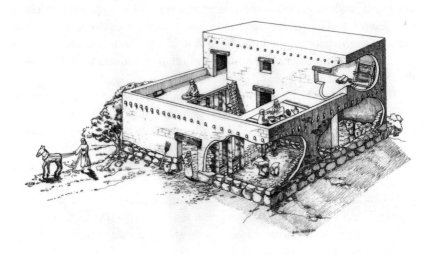

Reconstruction of a typical Iron Age Israelite/Judahite house

tecture. They are often equally spaced, sometimes within sight of each other. So these sites are related to other rural sites, not to the remaining Canaanite cities, mostly far distant on the coastal plain or in the inland valleys. There was no warfare, and no warfare was needed to settle the area, only perhaps a few local clashes.

(3) *House Type.* Domestic houses, almost more than anything else, can illuminate lifeways. It is significant that nearly all the hundreds of excavated Iron I hill country houses conform to a single type. A simple stone foundation and mudbrick structure is arranged in a sort of U-shaped plan, with a large, central, unroofed courtyard, flanked on both sides by several small rooms. Closely spaced rows of pillars suggest a second story.

The first floor features cooking facilities (a courtyard clay oven), storage rooms, and cobbled-surface rooms that were probably used as stables. Animals were safe there, their dung made for conveniently collectable fuel, and the heat they gave off warmed the second story. On the upper floor would have been sleeping quarters and perhaps a common room.

These houses range from six to twelve hundred square feet. Calculating about ten square feet of living space per person, based on Middle Eastern ethnographic parallels, each house may have accommodated anywhere from six to twelve persons.

The average size of a nuclear family in ancient Israel is estimated to have been between five and six members, since many children died in infancy. If we are dealing with extended, multigenerational families—a primary pair, plus a married son and his spouse and children—we arrive at the larger figure of as many as twelve people for a household. A few larger houses, especially those in the few small towns, may have had a servant or two (the Hebrew Bible even describes slaves).

These houses are often grouped in a circular pattern, forming a sort of perimeter ring that offers privacy and some protection. They also tend to share sidewalls, nested together and sharing common open spaces and courtyards. The impression is that of a closely knit family and kin-based social structure, strongly egalitarian in nature. This has been seen as reflecting a "patriarchal" society.

(4) *Social and Economic Structure.* Much of what we know of these subsystems has already been covered above. These are all rural villages in the hill country where the economy must have been based on a mixed strategy of farming and herding—a subsistence agropastoral economy. Each family would have been largely self-sufficient, even producing a small surplus for bartering. Based on ethnographic parallels, some women probably specialized in making pottery, and some men could have been builders or the like. Young people would have tended flocks in the nearby fields.

There may even have been a few shamans or cult functionaries. But there do not appear to have been any elites or professionals whatsoever. These were relatively isolated villages, with little or no contact with urban sites or authorities. The agrarian model described above fits best.

(5) *Political Structure.* Here our task is easy: there is none—at least no centralized authority, whether priestly, royal, or civil. At most, each village may have had a village elder, and at the clan level a sheikh-like chief may have held a hereditary office of sorts. At one time anthropologists and ethnographers were fond of postulating an evolutionary scheme that envisioned all societies progressing in a linear fashion from band, to tribe, to chiefdom, to state, but this scheme has proven too simplistic. All that is clear is that early Israel is neither a band, nor a tribe, nor a chiefdom; but it is not yet a state either.

(6) *Technology.* Not surprisingly, technology is as unsophisticated as the rural lifestyle. There is none of the elaborate bronze work of the Late Bronze Age, and little ironwork despite the label "Iron Age." Iron ore is scarce in Canaan; the smelting process is difficult and fuel-consumptive; and in any case, iron is brittle, rusts easily, and is not all that superior to bronze. The few metal implements we have are plow points, knives, chisels, and a few simple farm tools.

Houses never exhibit the fine ashlar, chisel-dressed masonry characteristic of earlier Canaanite sites and even some Phoenician sites now. Houses are of vernacular construction: low stone foundations, mudbrick walls, and a thatch and mud plastered roof. No architects or contractors were needed; each family built its own dwelling. There is no town planning, no city walls—only a sort of add-on arrangement of clusters of houses. There are absolutely none of the monumental palaces, temples, and administrative buildings that are typical of preceding Late Bronze Age Canaanite cities.

Two newly adapted technologies enhance the rural economy. Stone terraces are now developed into full-scale systems that convert rugged hillsides into stepped slopes suitable for small-scale agriculture—growing vegetables, fruits, olives, and especially grapes. The abundant rocks are scooped up and piled atop each other to build walls that conserve the thin soil and impede runoff of the winter rains along the narrow terraces. Without this extensive adaptation of earlier technology for a particular style of agriculture, settlement of the sparsely occupied hill country of Canaan would have been impossible.

Closely related to the requirements of agrarian life in the hill country are stone-lined silos for preserving wheat and barley. These serve not only to store the surpluses of each summer harvest, but also to tide people over during periodic droughts. One house at an Israelite village had more than forty such silos around it.

Finally, plastered cisterns dug deep into the limestone bedrock, which is everywhere near the surface, enable villages to store enough water to last through the long, dry summers, when it never rains. Lime plaster is known earlier, as are some rock-cut cisterns, but again, it is the adoption and combination of factors that represent a technological innovation, one particularly well suited to a rural economy.

It is pottery that distinguishes our early Israelite villages above all else. The ceramic repertoire continues Late Bronze Age traditions in general, providing us perhaps our best clue to local cultural identity. But many vessels are now handmade or hand-finished, rather than made on a fast wheel, as previously. This is a sort of "cottage industry." In addition, the statistics are different; there are virtually no luxury items, only utilitarian kitchen crockery. Store jars, cooking pots, and crude serving vessels predominate. There is no imported pottery from Greece or Cyprus, as previously, and, significantly, nothing whatsoever from Egypt.

(7) *Art and Aesthetics.* There is little or nothing of what we might call art in the early Israelite villages. We have none of the typical Late Bronze Age sculpture, ivory carving, jewelry, gem carving, bronzework, goldwork, silverwork, or anything else beyond the vernacular. We have only a few primitive stick-figure seals. There is not even any painted pottery.

Literacy

"Literacy" is defined as competency in using written language, i.e., the ability to read and write. Literacy may extend from simple "functional literacy," the ability to use a few words and numbers, all the way to the ability to deal with complex literary works.

In all premodern cultures, the majority of the population was illiterate, with only a few professional scribes being able to read and write. In ancient Israel, the adoption of the Old Canaanite alphabetic script made literacy more available by the eighth and seventh centuries BCE, but the majority were still illiterate.

One artistic expression to be considered is literature. From Late Bronze Age Canaan we have an extensive collection of literature in at least three languages and scripts: Akkadian written in a logosyllabic cuneiform script; Egyptian hieroglyphs; and the local Canaanite dialects written in early alphabetic scripts, both cuneiform and linear. We have hundreds of such texts, and many more must lie undiscovered underground.

From early Israel in the Iron I period we have only one inscription, a list of the letters of the thirty-character alphabet (known as an abecedary) in what is usually regarded as the "proto-Canaanite" script. It is clear that early Hebrew (and later biblical Hebrew as well) is a dialect of Canaanite, like the neighboring West Semitic languages of the Phoenicians, as well as Ammonites, Moabites, and Edomites in Transjordan. All these languages split off from Canaanite after its decline, and all used a variant of the alphabetic script popular then. This system made universal literacy possible in theory, since it was so simple. But the earliest Israelite society appears to have been almost entirely illiterate.

The discussion of one aspect of aesthetics—religion—will be delayed until Chapter 7. That is because we have almost no early Iron I evidence for any religious beliefs or practices. There are few if any shrines, certainly no temples, and no religious texts. Religion must have had a place in early Israelite society, as in every society that we have ever known. Nevertheless, we simply have no preserved evidence. The biblical texts, while dealing extensively with religion, were of course written centuries later. And their literary program of projecting Yahwism back to Moses at Mount Sinai cannot be uncritically accepted.

(8) *External Relations.* Here our discussion can be brief; aside from sporadic interaction with the nearby Philistines and Phoenicians, there are absolutely no external relations—not even with surviving local Canaanite towns and cities. The peoples of Transjordan are related to the Israelites much like

Ethnicity

The term "ethnicity" derives from the Greek *ethnos*, "people," thus "peoplehood." By ethnicity we mean the intellectual process by which an individual or society defines itself as distinct from others of the same potential class.

Many of what we call "ethnic traits" are factors of birth, which we cannot change. But others are the result of acculturation. Whatever the balance, the questions are (1) whether "ethnicity" is simply a construct; (2) whether there are any firm "ethnic boundaries"; and (3) whether we can recognize and define "ethnicity" on the basis of archaeological remains (i.e., without texts).

first cousins, but the biblical descriptions of contacts and ethnic conflicts with Transjordan are rather fanciful.

(9) *Ethnicity.* A final cultural and socioeconomic subsystem has to do not so much with substance as with perception—ethnicity. In short, how do we *know* that these Iron I hill country villages can be connected to the biblical Israelites? The archaeological assemblage, as we call it, has no labels.

The concept of "ethnicity" poses one of the most contentious issues that modern archaeology faces the world over. Skeptics, like the biblical revisionists discussed above, deny that we can say anything about ethnicity—certainly not on the basis of mere artifactual data, and not even when we have texts. As one scholar declared, "Ethnicity is hardly a common aspect of human existence at this very early period." Elsewhere, this scholar stated that ethnic markers are "accidental, even arbitrary."[3] In other words, the ancients—like our early Israelites—did not know (or care) who they were. Ethnicity is only a "social construct," in accordance with postmodernist ideology. That strains credulity.

The key is the notion of "ethnic markers"—characteristics that distinguish one group of people from another. What are these characteristics? Fredrik Barth, a distinguished Norwegian ethnographer, listed several of these characteristics in 1969. An ethnic group is a population or a people who:

1. Are biologically self-perpetuating.
2. Share a fundamental, recognizable, relatively uniform set of cultural values, including language.
3. Constitute a partly independent "interaction sphere."

3. Thomas L. Thompson, "Defining History and Ethnicity in the Southern Levant," pp. 168–87 in L. L. Grabbe, ed., *Can a 'History of Israel' Be Written?*, Journal for the Study of the Old Testament Supplement 245 (Sheffield: Sheffield Academic Press, 1997), 175.

4. Have a membership that defines itself, as well as being determined by others, as a category distinct from other categories of the same order.
5. Perpetuate their self-identity both by developing rules for maintaining ethnic boundaries as well as for participating in inter-ethnic social boundaries.

Is ethnicity then a "social construct"? Yes and no. Some essential ethnic traits, those of peoplehood, are genetic. Any individual's sense of self is partly the result of gender, birthplace, native language, and early acculturation. Other ethnic traits, however, are acquired and may fluctuate over time. Any American can become a European—multilinguistic and multicultural. But in the ancient world, such reinventions of one's self were nearly impossible.

So, what traits are different about early Israel? What *makes* them "Israelite"? Here we must operate on the assumption that things authentically reflect what their makers thought and how they behaved. Artifacts are the material correlates of thought and behavior. If so, they must reflect ethnicity, who people thought they were, and how they differed from others. It is all about identity and self-determination, and these are identifiable.

What then is different about our early Iron I hill country villages? Literally everything: settlement type and distribution, house form and family structure, lifestyle, ideology, almost everything that we can reconstruct on the basis of the archaeological data that we now have. Look at it this way: we can confidently identify Canaanites, Egyptians, Philistines, Phoenicians, Arameans, and others on the basis of their material culture remains *alone*. Why not Israelites?

The most secure evidence for Israelite ethnicity comes from cultural continuity. No one doubts that the archaeological evidence for a distinctive material culture by the Iron II period (ca. 1000–600 BCE) is "Israelite." After all, we have inscriptional evidence from neighboring countries that there *was* an "Israel" by the ninth century BCE. A Neo-Assyrian inscription of the ninth century BCE refers to the Israelite king Omri and acknowledges him as the king of Israel. The ninth-century BCE stele of Mesha, the king of Moab in Transjordan, refers to Omri and his son Ahab as kings of Israel. And the ninth-century-BCE Tel Dan inscription, found by Israeli archaeologists in 1993 at Tell Dan on the northern border, mentions a *dynasty* of David. It further specifies two kings we know from the Bible: Ahaziah of the southern kingdom and Jehoram of the northern kingdom. So by the ninth century BCE at the latest, Israel's neighbors recognized her as having a self-conscious ethnic identity.

The distinctive material culture of this Israel is even better documented in the Iron II period (ca. 1000–600 BCE; see Chapter 6). What is significant in the attempt to link ethnicity with material culture remains is that every single trait of Iron II Israel can be traced directly back to those of Iron I in an unbroken course of development.

The point is that if there is a distinct and recognizable "Israel" by the ninth century BCE, which no reasonable scholar doubts, then the predecessors of these late Israelites were *also* Israelites. These Iron I Israelites of the twelfth to eleventh centuries BCE were their authentic progenitors. Some scholars agree, but argue that in the interest of caution we should speak of these bearers of a new culture in Canaan as "Proto-Israelites."

It may be worth mentioning, however, that we do have corroborating textual evidence that is sometimes thought to be essential. The Merenptah inscription discussed above—dated precisely to the early Israelite horizon, ca. 1210 BCE—specifically refers to an "Israel" somewhere in Canaan. With the plural gentilic (people-specific hieroglyph) used in the Egyptian text, we should translate "the Israelite peoples," that is, a loosely affiliated group, in contrast to other peoples in Canaan regarded as city-states or nation-like entities.

Needless to say, the archaeologically attested Israel of the Iron I period that we have presented here fits the Israel of the Merenptah inscription precisely. Moreover, this Israel fits very well with the biblical depiction of Israel that we have reconstructed from the book of Judges (though not Joshua).

Thus we can identify Israel on the ground in Canaan a little before 1200 BCE, one that corresponds with both the archaeological evidence *and* a properly critical reading of the most relevant biblical accounts. As we have seen, these peoples were not invaders from Egypt or even Transjordan. They were mostly subsistence farmers and herders, seeking refuge from the chaos enveloping Canaan at the end of the Late Bronze Age.

On the highland frontier, previously sparsely inhabited, these newcomers could acquire land, secure their freedom, and establish a new lifestyle that our model here has called "agrarian." This really was the Israelites' promised land, notwithstanding its many perils.

For the later biblical writers, this all seemed miraculous. In fact, the emergence of early Israel in Canaan at this time does seem miraculous, even to us. The fact is that such a sweeping cultural change could have taken place *only* at this particular juncture of history. A century earlier, the Egyptians were still in control in Canaan, and by a century later too many other peoples were entrenched everywhere. Gaining a foothold for our homesteaders would have been difficult, if not impossible.

Scholars often speak of an "Axial Age"—an era when many intersecting factors create a crossroads from which one cannot turn back. History can be made by one fateful decision. Ancient Israel was born at one of the most critical crossroads in millennia—the end of the Bronze Age in the Levant.

So, early Israel was a product of the movements of indigenous people in Canaan, a socioeconomic upheaval rather than a foreign invasion. The archaeological evidence is overwhelming. The only question remaining for scholars today is *where* within Canaan? A few archaeologists still favor some variant of the "peaceful infiltration" model already discussed. They posit that the early hill country settlers were mostly pastoral nomads, perhaps the Shasu or other pastoralists well known from Transjordan. Or they may have been local pastoralists who now began to settle down and become farmers.

There are many reasons to question this scenario. For one thing, numerous ethnographic studies have shown that pastoral nomads tend to settle only when forced by central authorities to do so (as has happened in much of the Middle East in recent years). But in this instance, there was no central authority to enforce anything. The Egyptian authorities had decamped, leaving Canaan unpoliced.

Another force that can provoke a widespread movement of peoples is drought, which probably was one factor in the collapse that we have documented. But it seems unlikely that pastoral nomads would have chosen to become subsistence farmers during a time of prolonged drought. Remaining flexible and able to move to greener pastures would have been the better strategy for survival.

In any case, demography may be our best clue. There would have been only about twelve thousand people in the highlands of Canaan in the thirteenth century BCE. It is usually estimated that about ten percent of the population—that is, approximately twelve hundred—would have been pastoralists. Yet a century later, the population of the highland villages had grown to about forty to fifty thousand. If all the local pastoralists had settled down, we could not possibly account for such a population increase, not even if every woman bore several dozen children. There must have been a large influx of people from outside the local pastoral nomadic groups.

Many scholars look elsewhere for the pool from which we must draw, that is, among the settled population of Canaan. The most likely source would have been groups of refugees who were fleeing the decaying Canaanite enclaves along the coast and in the inland river valleys. These would have been urban dropouts; disenfranchised, landless people of all sorts; malcontents and social revolutionaries; adventurers and opportunists. The highland frontier would have been an attractive haven for all these peoples. If they do not seem to have had a lot in common, that should be no surprise. After all, the biblical account of the Hebrews departing out of Egypt says at the outset that they were a "mixed crowd," a motley crew.

One reason for seeking the roots of early Israel here is the fact that our highland settlers were farmers and stock-breeders, evidently long familiar with the challenges of agriculture in the harsh conditions of Canaan. Studies by experts in food production have shown that one early Israelite site was able to produce a sizable surplus from the very beginning. Pastoral nomads trying to survive would likely have starved to death their first winter (as the pilgrims did).

At another pertinent site, twenty-seven percent of the bones analyzed belonged to cattle. Nomads typically herd sheep and goats, but cattle are rarely herded because they are inefficient. They require a lot of pasture and water, and they cannot be herded seasonally over long distances. So, for archaeologists of most persuasions, our early Israelites look more like long-settled peoples from Canaan resettling themselves in the highlands, especially those taking refuge from the lowlands. If they had been farmers living in villages, small towns, or even commuting from cities to the fields, they would have been familiar with the local weather and conditions. They could have adapted easily and quickly to the hill country terrain. And they could have acquired land of their own— literally a matter of life and death in the preindustrial world. These settlers had a motive and a means.

Most biblical scholars today reject invasion hypotheses in favor of newer indigenous origins theories. But a few have questioned the exodus stories in the Bible even more radically than we have here. They argue that the grievous Egyptian bondage that the Israelites suffered did not take place in Egypt at all. It was rather in Canaan, in the Amarna Age ca. 1400–1300 BCE, which we discussed above, when local peoples were sorely oppressed by Egyptian authorities. That was really what was remembered, and it was the real-life context that influenced the story of liberation centuries later. Nevertheless, the setting of the biblical story is clearly in Egypt, not Canaan. The writers are determined: this was about Yahweh challenging the pharaoh in Egypt at the height of his power. While not named, the pharaoh from the exodus account could only have been one of Egypt's most powerful rulers, Ramesses II, who reigned from 1279–1213 BCE. He even campaigned far away in Syria, where he confronted the mighty Hittite armies and claimed to have defeated them.

What Is Left and Does It Matter?

Rewriting the emergence and the early history of Israel as we have done here, taking the archaeological data as primary, may appear to discredit the biblical account entirely and therefore to deprive it of meaning for modern readers.

On the contrary, we have only challenged the story of stupendous miracles in Exodus and Numbers and those of genocide in Joshua. The stories in Judges, by contrast, gain a new liveliness and relevance as we read them in their real-life archaeological context.

First, we learn how an obscure people can set out on the path to nation-hood, distinguishing themselves not by force of arms but through the force of their ideals—namely, the ideal of freedom and the dream of a better life for common folk. That belief, however naïve it may seem, also lives at the heart of the vision of America as the "New Israel."

But the dream can never be fully realized. We live amongst other peoples, who do not necessarily share our dream. Even the best, most promising leaders are often flawed. Heroes are mortal. Progress comes, but only in fits and starts. Even the promised land itself is perilous. Utopia remains beyond reach. Yet miracles can happen; how else to explain personal and national destiny? There may be something to call providence after all.

Furthermore, we learn that although the course of history is unpredictable, it is nevertheless always about moral choices. Thoughts and actions have consequences. Life has lessons. But the choices are in our hands; we make our own history, one way or another. It took ancient Israel two hundred years to carve out a place for itself in history, and failure, even extinction, threatened at every juncture. Israel may have been different, but it was not unique among the peoples of its day. We must always guard against exceptionalism, against triumphalism.

Finally, a strong centralized government or institutionalized clergy is not necessarily the *sine qua non*. The good life may be that of self-realizing individuals who tend to their families and live a simple life. They are in harmony with the rhythms of nature, loving the land and being good stewards of its riches. It is the *family* and its heritage, not the state, that is the basis of society and shapes the future. The archaeological record supports this picture of ordinary family life that is sometimes depreciated in the Bible, written as it was by the elites of society. That point is often overlooked.

One does not have to be the citizen of a great state. It is enough to be an honest, decent, caring person, living within one's means. The judges came and went, but the patrimonial family and clan remained the strength of ancient Israel in a time fraught with dangers. That strength in unity prevented the threat of dissolution that always loomed large.

Sometimes one must read the Bible "against the grain," to dispute the writers' opinions, to learn a negative lesson, as the medieval rabbis and others have done. The authors and editors of the book of Judges have obviously contrived a plot to set up their theme: the inevitability of a king appointed by Yahweh (which happens in the next book, Samuel). Hence their recurring pessimistic assessment that "in those days there was no king, and every man did what was right in his own eyes." They, of course, are the only ones who know what is "right." But even the biblical writers can be wrong. That is why populism is often so powerful in political discourse. The people do have a voice, and sometimes they can and should prevail.

It has been argued that despite the statist propaganda in some strands of the Hebrew Bible, a form of primitive democracy is at work from the earliest stages of Israel's history. It is a sort of egalitarianism, a protest against an authoritarian state. One of the several groups of reformers who arose from time to time to protest were called "Nazarites." Samson was a Nazarite; and in the New Testament John the Baptist appears like a Nazarite, a desert ascetic. These were zealous, prophet-like individuals who took radical vows. They fled the urban life, eschewed marriage, eked out a living in tents in the countryside, grew long hair and beards, and forswore wine and other luxuries. Most importantly, these dropouts from society considered themselves the *true* Israelites, not like the Canaanites. They were nostalgic, dreaming of a simpler past that may never have really existed. But they represented in stark form what has been called the biblical "nomadic ideal." Thus the old cry when urban life seemed too corrupt: "To your tents, O Israel!" Even so, most early Israelites had never lived in tents, certainly not in the Sinai wilderness. But the virtues of a simpler life, closer to nature, remained the ideal, never quite forgotten.

Let us return, however, to the *ordinary* people of ancient Israel, with whom we began. Given what we now know of the reality of life in early Israel, what did most people think and feel? And does that fit with the biblical portrait?

Most people were subsistence farmers, eking out a living in hamlets and small villages in the highlands. They were homesteaders, trying to gain a footing on the hill country frontier. Survivors of the collapse of millennia-old civilizations all around them, they wanted freedom, escape from the chaos, and a new life on new land.

Like most rural folk, these villagers would have been basically conservative, pragmatic, suspicious of elites and outside authority, and fiercely independent. They would have been deeply religious, but uninterested in theological formulations. Religion for them was what they felt worked to enhance their fundamental concern: survival. They were all illiterate. Even if the Bible had been written this early, they could not have read it. Its Hebrew would have been unintelligible to them; their dialect was closer to Canaanite. Their Bible was nature, their calendar its rhythms. Their Sinai covenant, the Ten Commandments, the Passover celebration, temple theology—these were all later literary constructs, and they were not part of their experience of the world, of the good and proper life.

It doesn't take much imagination to see that this early Israelite worldview fits amazingly well with our archaeological portrait. It also fits the portrait of life in the books of Judges and Samuel during the days of the judges "when everyone did what was right in their own eyes." The biblical writers repeat that refrain mostly to set up their justification of kingship, yet it reflects the views of the majority.

The portrait in the book of Joshua of Israel's mighty army vanquishing the whole Canaanite population would have been unknown and unimaginable to these Proto-Israelites. They knew better: the Canaanites were still around, and their strategy for survival was different. For them, the promised land was their struggle to secure their own small plot of land, to make a living from it, and to pass it on to their children.

CHAPTER 5

Yahweh Comes to the Rescue: Divine Kingship

The Biblical Narrative

The book of Judges ends with the complaint that there was no king in Israel in those days, so people just did as they pleased (Judg. 21:25). That was deplorable. But now there is a real crisis: there are Philistines at the door.

Samuel, the main character of the book bearing his name, is the last of the judges and the first of the prophets. The prophets (Hebrew *nabi'*) are those who speak for Yahweh, not necessarily to predict, but to interpret God's will for the moment. Some two hundred years have passed since Israel's first successful settlement in the hill country. While she has expanded, so have the Philistines along the coastal plain, and they are now attempting to press inland into Judah. Samuel was dedicated to Yahweh's service at his birth because he was a miracle child. His mother Hannah had not been able to conceive, but Yahweh answered her fervent prayers at the shrine of Shiloh, an old tribal center.

Her son Samuel seemed destined to serve as a priest at Shiloh, and his fame grew as he did. But Yahweh appeared to him and commissioned him for a new role. The Philistines had encamped at Aphek, on the border at the headwaters of the Yarkon River. The Israelites had stationed themselves at nearby Ebenezer. They had been soundly defeated in battle and lost four thousand men. The route up into the heartland of Judah now lay open. What to do? In desperation, the Israelites go up to the shrine of Shiloh to retrieve the old ark of the covenant (which had been preserved there) representing the presence of Yahweh among his people. They resolve to take it into battle to help ensure victory. The Philistines are dismayed, but again they prevail, this time killing 30,000 of Israel's men. The Philistines seize the ark and carry it off to Ashdod, where they set it up in the temple of Dagon. Two sons of the priest Eli—Hophni and Phinehas—perish in the conflict.

Ironically, the ark turns out to be more of a nuisance than a treasure for the Philistines, so they decide to return it to Beth-Shemesh on the Israelite border. The return of the ark ushers in an era of peace, or perhaps more likely a détente.

In Samuel's old age, he is confronted by the elders of Israel, who are worried that his wayward sons may succeed him (1 Sam. 8). They demand: "Give us a king to judge us like all the nations" (1 Sam. 8:5). Samuel is reluctant and prays to Yahweh, who says to let them have their king, since they have rejected him. Yahweh alludes to his deliverance of the Israelites from Egypt, whereupon the children of Israel had pledged him their allegiance.

Samuel reluctantly goes back to the elders, but he warns them about the consequences of what they are asking. A king will draft their sons into the army, he will set up a military aristocracy, he will confiscate their harvests, he will enslave their daughters, he will rob them all of everything. Then, Samuel says, they will cry out in dismay, but Yahweh will turn a deaf ear. Undeterred, the elders insist that only a king will go out to fight their battles. Although the Philistines are not specifically named in this story, it is clear that they are the principal threat.

Curiously, there are two accounts of Samuel's reaction to the institution of kingship. The dual account no doubt reflects two or more older sources that the writers of the books of Samuel have skillfully edited together. The writers must have seen the contradiction, but because they knew from their own day how problematic the institution of kingship could be they let both accounts stand. In the alternative version (1 Sam. 9) Samuel has no hesitation. He willingly selects an anonymous young man from the territory of Benjamin named Saul, who was out tending his father's donkeys. At Yahweh's instruction, Samuel anoints Saul as king over Israel. The rationale? The young man is exceptionally tall and robust with the glow of health about him.

Saul calls all the people of Israel together at Mizpah, near Jerusalem, and declares that Yahweh will yet deliver them from the Philistines, even though they have betrayed him by seeking out other gods. Saul, with no experience or qualifications to rule, begins his reign at Gibeah, a small hilltop site within view of Jerusalem. Jerusalem is not yet destined to be the capital, although now we have a rudimentary state. Or do we?

A pivotal point of departure has been reached. Israel has moved almost imperceptibly from the charismatic leadership of the judges to a hereditary institutional kingship. There will be no turning back, and the monarchy will sometimes be unstable for the next four hundred years. But the biblical writers legitimate kingship as a divinely ordained and sanctified office.

When Saul, probably little more than a teenager, has been on the throne only two years, he sets out with three thousand men against the Philistines at Geba (an unknown site). The Philistines field six thousand men and three thousand chariots. Despite divisions within his ranks, with Yahweh's help Saul defeats the Philistine army and drives the remainder of their forces back to the coastal plain. Saul then campaigns against Ammon, Moab, and Edom in Transjordan, and even into Syria, where the Aramean city-states are now burgeoning.

But all is not well, so much so that Yahweh admits to Samuel that he is sorry to have selected Saul. The Philistines are able to regroup, and they muster at the mouth of the Elah Valley leading up to Jerusalem. The Israelites draw up on the north side of the valley, the Philistines on the opposite side. A famous battle takes place where a young David kills the giant Goliath. The lad seems to have appeared from nowhere, but Samuel has already anointed him as a future king, because he knows that Saul is in disfavor with Yahweh.

Saul continues his war against the Philistines, but David does not join him, although his older brothers do. Saul gives his beloved daughter Michal to David as his wife, so David now becomes the king's son-in-law, though he is not in the line of succession. Already, one sees young David's cunning; he will soon drive the old man out of his mind.

David is uncommonly appealing, and his fame grows day by day. Among his many gifts, he is a musician, and he uses his talents to amuse Saul. Saul is increasingly depressed, however, and on the edge of madness ("an evil spirit was upon him"). He begs young David to calm him by playing his lyre, but in a jealous rage he loses his temper and hurls a javelin at him. Michal helps him flee to Samuel, where he is shielded, but he is now in exile.

Showing his wiliness again, David goes over to the Philistines as a mercenary and deliberately challenges Saul. After Samuel's death, David feigns loyalty, and Saul welcomes him back as his own son. Eventually, Saul sets out for battle one last time to meet the Philistines on Mount Gilboa in Galilee. He is severely wounded, and, fearful that he will fall into Philistine hands alive, he asks his armor-bearer to kill him. When he refuses, Saul falls upon his own sword. His three sons, including Jonathan, David's bosom friend (much has been made of this), are all killed. David was not there that day. Just his good fortune?

By our calculations, Saul came to the throne somewhere around 1020 BCE and reigned no more than twenty years. David succeeds him, even though he is not the legitimate heir. His will be a reign like no other. In reality a serial killer, as some scholars have maintained, he is remembered as "a man after God's own heart." When the messenger brings him the good news (!) of Saul's death on Mount Gilboa, David kills him (as though he is really angry). Abner, Saul's chief of staff, unreconciled to David's takeover, installs Saul's remaining son Ish-bosheth—whose name means "man of shame"—as a rival king in Gilead in Transjordan.

The other sons of Saul who are still living are at war with David. Abner, a military commander serving Saul's successor, Ish-bosheth, surprisingly appeals to David at Hebron. David receives him and gives him a feast; but then Joab, his general, kills Abner. Thereupon David puts on a great show of grief, following Abner's bier to the grave and ordering all the people to mourn with him. His stock rises in the eyes of all. He is Yahweh's anointed, and he is acting nobly.

Ish-bosheth, Saul's son and David's rival, is killed by his own henchmen. When these fellows bring his head to David, who should have been relieved, he slaughters them, cuts off their hands and feet, and hangs their bodies by the pool in Hebron. All his rivals are now conveniently removed, revenge heaped upon his enemies.

Emboldened, David leaves his stronghold at Hebron behind and sets his eyes on Jerusalem, a town held by the Jebusites, evidently old Canaanite loyalists. He takes the town by a clever ruse. The city, set on a hill, is defended by a formidable city wall. But David and his men find the place where a conduit (the biblical *tsinnor*) leads from the spring in the Kidron Valley below, under the walls, and up into the city (2 Sam. 5:7–9). They creep through the dark, narrow passageway up into the city, surprising the guards and opening the city gates for the waiting troops. The city miraculously falls into David's hands, and he dubs it modestly the "City of David." The name will stick for three thousand years. It is another sign that David's dynasty is divinely blessed and will rule forever.

Jonathan, Saul's son, had had a son who was named Mephibosheth because he was crippled (Hebrew *bosheth* meaning "shame"), a handicap thought in those days to be a sign of Yahweh's disfavor. David learns about him and has him brought before him. Mephibosheth begs for mercy, and David promises to spare him for the sake of his father Jonathan, David's beloved companion.

David shelters Mephibosheth for some time, but then kills the five sons of his estranged wife, Saul's daughter Michal. David feigns grief and protests his loyalty. He retrieves the remains of Saul and Jonathan and gives them an honorable burial in their homeland in Benjamin (2 Sam. 21:12–14). David not only pursues the war against the Philistines (whom he once served), but now he campaigns up into Syria as far as Zobah, 150 miles north of Damascus, encountering the Aramean king Hadadezer. But at home he courts disaster, literally.

David spies a beautiful woman bathing on the roof of a house near the palace. He has her brought to him and begins an adulterous affair. Bathsheba becomes pregnant, but she is married to Uriah, a soldier in David's army. David orders Uriah back, plies him with wine, and sends him home to Bathsheba. He hopes that Uriah will have intercourse with her so that Uriah will think the child is his and the deception can be pulled off. But poor Uriah falls asleep on his doorway and never beds his wife. David orders Uriah back to the front, giving covert instructions to Joab to retreat and leave him helpless. Not surprisingly, Uriah is killed, whereupon David installs his widow in the palace.

The prophet Nathan—the first to speak truth to power—accuses David by means of a parable. A rich man, he says, had many flocks, but he stole the one lamb a poor man had. David says in effect: "Who would do such a thing?" Nathan declares: "You are the man!"

Yahweh will spare David, says Nathan, but the illegitimate child is cursed. When the baby becomes ill and dies, David is heartbroken and seems repentant. He comforts Bathsheba (so to speak), and she bears another child whose name is Solomon. He will be a legitimate heir to the throne.

Despite these various misadventures, which the people always seem to forgive, David does give some attention to administration. He carries out a census (how better to tax his subjects?) and levies a *corvée* or forced conscription of labor. He aspires to build a temple to house the ark of the covenant. A palace and a temple would embellish his capital and make him a visible rival to the Aramean kings. But Nathan informs David that despite being indulged by Yahweh, he is a "man of war" and thus cannot be allowed to construct a temple, a monument to peace.

David has not disposed of all his rivals, however. His own son, Absalom ("Father of Peace"), plots against him. David hears of this and sends forces to counter the rebellion, cautioning his general Joab to "deal gently with the young man" (2 Sam. 18:5). But Absalom gets caught in a tree and is struck to death by Joab and his commanders. His body is then thrown into a pit, and stones are piled on top. When the news is brought to David, he cries, "Oh my son Absalom, if only I had died instead!" (2 Sam. 18:33). He seems inconsolable, but all along he must have known what would happen when he sent Joab to confront Absalom.

David, the man raised up by Yahweh as his own anointed, a messiah, the "sweet psalmist of Israel," dies at an old age, having reigned a disputed forty years. His son Adonijah was supposed to succeed him, but on his deathbed David selects Solomon and charges him to "keep all the commandments of Moses." Nevertheless, he urges Solomon to avenge him by killing Joab, who had allowed Absalom to die.

The long and complex story of David—sometimes called "the Court History of David"—occupies the whole of 2 Samuel. It is almost a complete novella inserted into the epic Deuteronomistic History that extends from the book of Deuteronomy through Kings. It is equaled only by the saga of Moses in Exodus. It was probably composed in the seventh century BCE, using a number of earlier sources. It is a heroic yet tragic tale.

Baruch Halpern's magnificent analysis is entitled *David's Secret Demons: Messiah, Murderer, Traitor, King* (2001). According to Halpern, David was "a serial killer," all the while masquerading as Yahweh's anointed. How did he get by with it? Or did he? What are we to make of such an accomplished but deeply flawed man? Can archaeology help?

Before we turn to the archaeological evidence, let us try to explain how David attained his enduring fame. What did he actually accomplish? Not much, it turns out. His pushing the Philistines back to the coastal plain, where they remained confined until the invasion of the Babylonians in 605 BCE, may have been his greatest achievement. Apart from that, 2 Samuel and 1 Kings flesh out their narrative with dramatic personal stories that may be colorful but appear to be the stuff of legend. Certainly they cannot be confirmed by archaeology.

It may be that the reason the Hebrew Bible elevates David to almost god-like status is that for them the temple in Jerusalem was paramount; it was the symbol of Yahweh's abiding presence among his covenant people. And the continuity of the Davidic dynasty was the best guarantee that the temple, built by David's successor, would survive eternally.

Let us turn now to David's son and successor, Solomon. In contrast to David, Solomon's story seems like a breath of fresh air. He is a wise, just, and God-fearing king. Solomon also ruled some forty years, and since he inherited a kingdom now largely at peace he could devote himself to administration and even to the arts. Among his many artistic pursuits, Solomon was said to have been the author of three thousand proverbs and many of the poems in the book of Psalms. He was fabled as an extraordinarily learned philosopher, the wisest man in the world. He was rich as Croesus; everything he touched turned to gold. Foreign potentates like the queen of Sheba heard of his fame and visited him.

But his greatest achievement was the building of the temple of Yahweh in Jerusalem. There had never been anything like it. Since Israel had no tradition of monumental architecture, Solomon imported materials from Phoenicia and hired architects and masons from Hiram, king of Tyre. So great was Solomon's wealth that the yearly tributes to him included 660 talents of gold (some 5,000 lbs.). He supported his extravagant realm by continuing David's policy of *corvée* or enforced labor. He also enslaved the remaining non-Israelites in his kingdom. In addition to constructing a monumental temple, Solomon built other structures on the fortified hill of Jerusalem. These included an administrative complex; a hall of justice; and a harem for his legendary seven hundred wives and three hundred concubines. He also rebuilt David's *millo* (Hebrew "filling, terrace").

Similar royal acropolis foundations have been found at Syro-Hittite or Aramean sites in Syria and Anatolia. Especially close are those at Tell Halaf and Zinjirli (ancient Samaal). These ninth- to eighth-century royal cities feature a lower city, then an upper, walled compound that incorporates the palace, administrative buildings, and a small temple.

Among Solomon's many wives was one of Pharaoh's daughters, given along with her dowry. That dowry consisted of, among other things, the city of Gezer, which the pharaoh had captured and "burned with fire." In a famous passage in 1 Kings 9:15–17, Solomon is said to have fortified (Hebrew *banah*, "to build" or "rebuild") four sites as royal cities: Gezer, Megiddo, Hazor, and of course Jerusalem, his capital. Then he is said to have ruled for forty years, like his father, David.

Above all, Solomon solidified the line of succession, and the dynasty of David continued on the throne of Jerusalem for three hundred more years. Even more so than David, Solomon was a successful monarch by the standards of his day. Though he was greatly admired, however, it was David who remained the ideal king.

At Solomon's death, civil war broke out, and his son Rehoboam took the throne in Judah, while Jeroboam siezed control in the north. Thus the so-called "united kingdom" (the Hebrew Bible does not use the term) came to an end after a little more than a century, and the country remained divided into a southern kingdom of Judah and a northern kingdom of Israel. The Davidic dynasty survived only in Judah (see Chapter 6).

An Archaeological Critique

The biblical stories of Saul, David, and Solomon are obviously "tall tales," at least in part. Can archaeology bring them down to earth a bit? The answer is yes to a surprising degree.

Let us start with Saul's reign. We know little about it from external evidence, since his reign was short and his modest projects have left few material remains. A date of ca. 1020 BCE for his accession is calculated based on the biblical claim that Solomon and David each reigned for forty years (if reliable). The date of ca. 930 BCE for Solomon's death is based on the biblical notation that his death occurred five years before the Egyptian pharaoh "Shishak"—clearly Shoshenq of the Twenty-Second Dynasty, who died in 924 BCE—raided Judah in 925 BCE (1 Kgs. 15:25). Adding eighty years, we get 1010 BCE for Saul's death.

The narrative of Saul's humble background as a shepherd of the tribe of Benjamin, north of Jerusalem, fits quite well with the rural society and family structure that we now know and have already seen in Judges. When Saul becomes king, he establishes himself in a fortress at Gibeah. That site has been identified with a small but prominent hilltop three miles north of Jerusalem named Tell el-Ful.

The site was excavated by the great American archaeologist Albright, who in 1922–1923 brought to light a tower that he interpreted as part of a rectangular fortress built on bedrock. Further excavations in the 1960s suggested that Albright's "rude fortress" of Saul was not very impressive. But one would not expect it to have been.

The "thirty thousand chariots" attributed to Saul is certainly a vast exaggeration; there is no archaeological evidence for chariotry at all in this period. Saul's "six thousand" armed men is more realistic in the light of our estimate of a total population of about seventy-five thousand at the time.

Military campaigns into Transjordan are not likely, since these entities were still not state-like at the time and would have posed no threat to the fledgling kingdom of Judah. These entities did exist, however, as current archaeological evidence demonstrates.

Further campaigns into Syria as far as Zobah, some 150 miles north of Damascus, are not supported. The Aramean tribes there are known to have been settled into several city-states by now, but Israelite exploits that far afield are not credible, nor would there have been any reason for them.

The story of David and Goliath and the battle of Elah Valley will be postponed until later. The epic tale of Saul's death atop Mount Gilboa fighting the

Philistines from Beth Shean is almost certainly fictitious. The biblical Philistines along the coast are well known in this period, as we have seen, but they never penetrated that far north or that far inland. There were a handful of Philistine potsherds found at Beth Shean, but by now the site is largely an abandoned Egyptian fort, occupied by a few remaining Canaanites. Furthermore, the remote heights of Mount Gilboa are no place for a pitched battle. That would have taken place more likely in the Jezreel Valley below, especially if Saul's reputed chariots were involved. Iron chariots could never have maneuvered up the steep slopes of Mount Gilboa, more than 1700 ft. above sea level. Other campaigns and victories against the Philistines may be more realistic, but they are not documented. In the light of the archaeological evidence, Saul's brief reign can be seen as possibly historical in general, but not corroborated in any detail.

The evidence for David as king is much more substantial. First, there is extrabiblical evidence that a "King David" actually lived, against the assertion of some skeptics that King David is no more real than King Arthur. In 1993 a large stone slab was found incorporated in a rebuilt ninth-century outer gateway at Tel Dan, on the northern border. It turned out to have a partially preserved inscription in Aramaic, a sister language of Hebrew.

It is a "victory stele" of the Aramaic king Hazael, who is celebrating a victory over "Jehoram son of Ahab, king of Israel" and "Ahaziah son of Jehoram, king of the house of David" (filling in a few breaks).

Some of the biblical revisionists (see Chapter 1) immediately declared the stele a modern forgery; it was inconvenient for their theories. But all experts have affirmed its authenticity. There is no doubt that the names of the two kings are the same as those known in the Bible. And if one or the other belongs to a Davidic dynasty (as Jehoram does), then there was an earlier founder named "David."

The inscription is a bit later, partially broken, and was found in secondary use as rubble in a stone wall. But it shows beyond doubt that David was remembered as a king and was well known to Israel's neighbors by the mid-ninth century BCE, not long after Solomon's death.

Yet "proof" has its difficulties. Here we have a rare case of two parallel versions of an incident: the biblical one in Hebrew and the Aramaic one. In the biblical account our Jehoram, the king of northern Israel, is killed in a military coup led by the renegade general Jehu (2 Kgs. 9). But in the Tel Dan stele, it is the Aramean king Hazael, well known from other inscriptions (and the Bible) who kills Jehoram. Both stories cannot be true, so which is it? We could suppose that the version that has the least reason for spinning the story is

The Tel Dan Inscription

the better one. But both the Israelites and the Arameans had good reasons for their own propaganda (that's what royal inscriptions are). The biblical writers disapprove of the bothersome Omri-Ahab dynasty because it is not of the Davidic line. So they celebrate the victory of the rebel Jehu; he avenges David and the Yahwists. However, the Arameans naturally claim a victory over their arch-enemy Israel, vindicating their king Hazael. There the historian must leave matters.

David's focus on Jerusalem as his new capital is understandable. An old Jebusite enclave, it is situated on three high hills, fairly defensible and in "neutral" territory in central Judah, and relatively well watered by springs. Furthermore, Jerusalem may not have been heavily occupied in the thirteenth to eleventh centuries BCE, as we know. The way David and his men were able to sneak into the walled city through a water conduit has been discussed above. It is tempting to connect the biblical reference to one of several water systems in Jerusalem that have been investigated since the nineteenth century. The most likely candidate for David's *tsinnor* is the so-called "Warren's Shaft" (named after its nineteenth-century explorer, Sir Charles Warren). This is a steep, narrow, vertical shaft cut through the bedrock, leading from the Gihon Spring in the valley horizontally under the city wall and then vertically up into the city. Recent examination by spelunkers, expert rock-cave climbers, shows that while the shaft was meant to be invulnerable, it was not. Difficult, but not impossible. Thus the story of David's miraculous capture of the city of Jerusalem is by no means fantastic.

The old Jebusite city would have had a city wall, no doubt having been repaired after an earlier Canaanite destruction by now. Such a later city wall around the slopes of the City of David is in fact known. David's palace was probably a fortified complex, a citadel like those well known in contemporary sites in Syria and Turkey (above). South of the Temple Mount in Jerusalem a monumental, multi-room stone structure with walls as much as fifteen feet thick, founded on bedrock, has been discovered. Called the "large stone structure," it is badly ruined and only partially preserved. Some potsherds below the thin surfaces definitely do date to the tenth century BCE, but nothing remains on the floor. The excavator regards this structure as the "citadel of David," built with Phoenician help (2 Sam. 5:11). Other scholars are less certain, and some are altogether skeptical.

David is said to have built the *millo*. The Hebrew term *millo* comes from a verb meaning "to fill." It is presumed to refer to a sort of artificial fill, such as built-up stone terraces. A large stone-terraced slope south of the Temple Mount, known since the last century and excavated several times, is very likely to be what the biblical writers mean by their *millo*. It may have been first constructed in the thirteenth century BCE, but it was rebuilt several times later. It would have been essential to the buildup of a densely occupied city

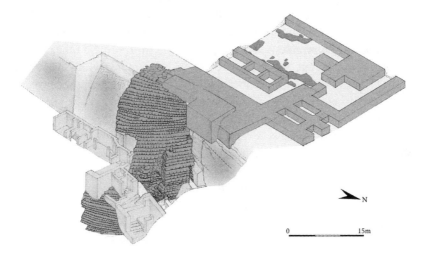

"Stepped stone structure" in Jerusalem

on the Ophel slopes, by consolidating the hillside and allowing for step-like houses to be closely grouped. The upper houses would have used the roof of the next lower ones as a terrace, and so on. Several Iron Age houses have been excavated atop this so-called "stepped stone structure." They were destroyed in the Babylonian destruction in 586 BCE, but they may have been constructed centuries earlier as is often the case. This, then, would have been the "City of David," relatively well attested.

David, like Saul, is said to have campaigned as far north as Zobah in Syria, but we have shown above how unlikely that is. His protracted war against the Philistines, however, can readily be documented. Although few scholars have ever attempted it, one can look at the dozens of excavated ethnic Israelite and Philistine sites along the supposed border in Judah. Then if we line up the relevant strata (or layers) of all these sites, opposite one another, a real border can be mapped. Furthermore, it can be shown that nearly all the Philistine sites do attest disturbances and destructions in the mid-tenth century BCE, after which they are permanently diminished. That is good evidence that David not only fought these wars, but won most of them.

Even more decisive evidence comes from recent excavations at Tell Qeiyafa, a site on the border with Philistia, overlooking the Valley of Elah where the famous battle of David and Goliath was fought. The isolated hilltop has a magnificent view over the valley and to Philistia beyond. It is essentially a one-period site, dated by pottery and other considerations, such as radiocarbon dates, to the early tenth century BCE (even skeptics agree on the date). The site was heavily fortified by a city wall running as much as a mile around the perimeter and incorporating some two hundred tons of stones. The site has two three-way entry gates that are typical of the Iron Age. No other known site has more than one. Qeiyafa may therefore be identified with "Shaarayim" in the Hebrew Bible, the name meaning "two gates." That site is portrayed as being somewhere in the vicinity of the Valley of Elah.

Qeiyafa exhibits a town plan that was common in Judah, especially at cities that were constructed as royal administrative centers like Beth-Shemesh, Mizpah, and Beersheba. A double wall runs around the periphery, with houses built into the wall. This is not a vernacular town or village, but rather a "barracks town," deliberately constructed to face Philistines on the other side of the valley and defend against them.

Such a well-planned, heavily fortified, fully provisioned site in a formidable border setting cannot have been constructed by a group of farmers and villagers. It must have been deliberately planned and constructed by a centralized authority. But by whom? Given the secure early tenth-century date, the only candidate is David, well organized in his capital of the Judean kingdom in Jerusalem.

The biblical authors of the books of Kings were writing some two or three centuries after the time of David, and their work is obviously in part propaganda glorifying their champion's glorious reign. But they seem to have had good sources—perhaps a lost document called the "Court History of David" mentioned in the biblical text. Of course the many colorful details of David's personal life and of his reign cannot be corroborated. But the skepticism of some about the essential historicity of the biblical account cannot be justified, nor for that matter can doubts about theological inferences to be drawn from the stories.

As though this were not evidence enough, Qeiyafa has produced some evidence of literacy. Three inscriptions in a variant of an early Canaanite-like script (Hebrew being written in a variant of that script) have been found there. One of them is a very well executed inscription chiseled into a storage jar. One name is *Ish-Baal*, "Man of (the god) Baal." This is the first time that such a Hebrew name has been found outside the Bible. There it occurs as the name of one of Saul's sons, who attempted to rule before David rose to power (1 Chr. 8:33). In 2 Samuel, however, we find a different name for the same individual: *Ish-bosheth*, "Man of shame" (2 Sam. 2:10). The change is no doubt due to the fact that the old Canaanite God Baal was denounced by the biblical writers, so they changed this person's name: not "Man of Baal," but "Man of shame." Yet the fact that this name occurs in the Hebrew Bible only in the contexts of the Davidic era suggests that at Qeiyafa it may refer to the biblical Ish-bosheth. That fits the date of Qeiyafa precisely, and the advancement of literacy is a hallmark of early state development.

We turn now to the reign of Solomon. Even a casual reader will conclude that the biblical story of "Solomon in all his glory" is replete with many exaggerations. He rules a kingdom from the border of Egypt to the Euphrates river. He has a thousand wives and concubines. He conscripts thirty thousand laborers; for the construction of the temple he has seventy-eight thousand workers and thirty-three hundred supervisors. His army boasts twelve thousand horses and fourteen hundred chariots. His annual tribute in gold amounts to five thousand pounds. He carries out extensive trade with southern Arabia, and the queen of Sheba visits him and acknowledges his greatness. He is the wisest man in the world.

Solomon's chariot force is without archaeological confirmation, since the buildings first interpreted as stables at Megiddo have now been questioned. In any case, it is agreed that these structures belong to the ninth century BCE and reflect Ahab's reign. Some trade with south Arabia is now documented, and the biblical reference to spices as part of that trade fits the evidence that we have. The kingdom of a people known as the Sabeans is known to have existed in south Arabia by the eighth century BCE. That would mean that the story of the visit of a queen of Sheba may rest on some historical events (although a female ruler would have been an anomaly).

The Phoenician connections in the accounts of Solomon's reign do seem realistic in general. The Phoenicians were Iron Age contemporaries of the Israelites, heirs of the old Bronze Age Canaanite culture, now restricted mainly to the northern coast of Israel and the Lebanon coast. Their language and script are very close to those of ancient Israel. Having both better natural anchorages and easily accessible timber (the famous "cedars of Lebanon"), the Phoenicians became legendary maritime traders. They planted trading colonies in North Africa and even in far-off Spain. That Solomon would have found them desirable trading partners is not necessarily derived from legend. The biblical account of Solomon's reign tells us how he worked with the Phoenicians in two regards. His collaboration with Hiram, king of Tyre, in engaging in naval operations and trade via Eilat on the Red Sea is problematic. The presumed port of Ezion-geber has been excavated and is a fort, not actually on the seacoast; and there is nothing there earlier than the eighth or possibly the ninth century BCE. The interaction with Ophir is problematic, since its location is unknown. But perhaps it was somewhere down the Red Sea toward the southern Arabian coast where we have already discussed the possibility of trade. We do have an ostracon, an inscribed piece of pottery, found long ago at Tell Qasile near Tel Aviv, that reads "gold of Ophir, for Beth-Horon, 30 shekels." But the port of Tel Aviv, which would have been Jaffa, would not have had access to Ophir if it were down the Red Sea somewhere. And the ostracon is later in date.

Solomon's dream of erecting a monumental temple in Jerusalem required him to look abroad for architects and builders, since Israel had no traditions of such architecture. Going to the nearby Phoenicians was the best option, because they were ship builders and familiar with timbers. There was also a long tradition in Phoenicia and Syria of working with the fine chisel-dressed masonry that we call "ashlar." The palace at the famous port city of Ugarit, dating from the fourteenth to thirteenth centuries BCE, is constructed of superb ashlar masonry.

It is noteworthy that Phoenician-style ashlar masonry is common in tenth-century constructions in Israel, such as the city gates and other structures at sites like Megiddo and Gezer. Of course we do not possess any remains of the

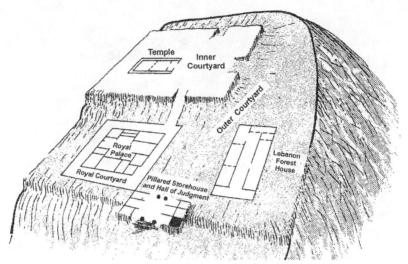

Reconstructed plan of the Temple Mount and nearby monumental structures

Jerusalem temple. But the biblical descriptions of the masonry, presumably Phoenician, fit known ashlar masonry in detail.

The accounts in 1 Kings 5:17; 6:7; 7:9, 10 describe large stones cut to measure and dressed, pre-fitted at the quarry so that when later installed on the Temple Mount "not a sound was heard." At Megiddo, Samaria, and Gezer precisely such dressed ashlar masonry is found. And at both Megiddo and Gezer in the tenth century BCE, identical mason's marks are seen, clearly guides for assembly. At Megiddo, some of the blocks still showed the red marks of chalk-lines used in cutting and finishing the masonry.

Further evidence for Solomon's reputed "Golden Age" is relatively abundant, but sometimes more controversial. By now well entrenched on his fortified acropolis in Jerusalem, the new capital, Solomon moves to carry out what seems to reflect a preconceived notion of what a Levantine state capital should look like. The combination of a lower walled city, crowned by a walled acropolis with its own palace, administrative structures, and a temple/royal chapel, is well attested at Neo-Hittite or Aramean sites in Syria and Turkey.

Two such excavated ninth-century-BCE sites—Zinjirli (ancient Sam'al) and Tell Halaf—exhibit precisely this combination of architectural elements. That was what Solomon wanted to imitate: other sites that by comparison give a clear statement of his claim to be a legitimate dynastic king, the equal of any.

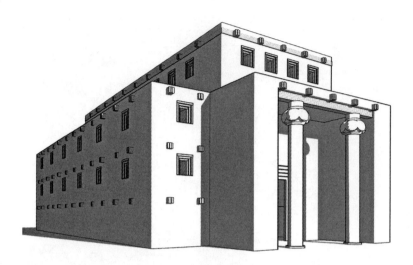

Reconstruction of Solomon's temple

"Solomon's temple" has often been dismissed as about as fanciful as Midas's touch. Is there any archaeological evidence for such an elaborate building, even if Solomon himself was a really historical character? It turns out that there is.

A generation or so ago, the temple in Jerusalem, described in great detail in 1 Kings 6–8, loomed large in our imagination. That is because it was thought to be unique, and therefore poorly appreciated as a real structure with believable furnishings. There were no parallels elsewhere in the ancient Near East, and certainly nothing like this in Israel.

Today that has all changed. We know of two dozen or more similar temples from all over the ancient East, particularly Syria. They are constructed on the same plan. They are rectangular buildings with a single doorway and three rooms, arranged in a straight line, focused on an altar on the back wall of the innermost room. Some have a portico-like entrance that may have two supporting columns. That is precisely what the biblical description of Solomon's temple looks like.

One recently excavated temple at Ain Dara in northern Syria, dated to the ninth to eighth century BCE, provides at least a dozen almost exact parallels to the Solomonic temple in Jerusalem. It features a tripartite plan, two columns flanking the entrance, a backroom altar, side halls, triple-recessed windows, and winged cherubs (human-headed lions or bulls). The decorations include latticework and twisted-rope designs. All these elements are described in detail in the Bible.

Elsewhere there are many parallels. The portable wheeled bronze braziers used in the Jerusalem temple to provide heat and light have nearly identical Phoenician parallels in Cyprus. Their decorations include birds, bulls, cherubs, flowers, and chain-like motifs, and the wheels are spoked. That accords almost exactly with descriptions in the Bible of such braziers.

Most of the temples are in essence royal chapels, monumental buildings constructed by the palace and situated nearby, serviced by the official priesthood. That is what the Jerusalem temple was. Although it becomes a symbol of national status—of the people of Israel—few had ever seen it. Probably none had ever entered the temple, since only the king and high priest were permitted, and in the inner chamber only the high priest.

The intricate details in the biblical description are difficult to grasp, because some of the Hebrew terms are rare, and a few occur only here. The reason for the obscure language is undoubtedly the fact that the biblical authors were writing some two or three centuries after the construction of the building. They probably had earlier sources, but the technical terms for the construction and the furnishings would have been unfamiliar to them. After all, they were not architects, masons, or artisans. If the biblical tradition is taken seriously, that Solomon imported the design and the workers from Phoenicia, then the biblical writers were working with foreign concepts and a remote dialect.

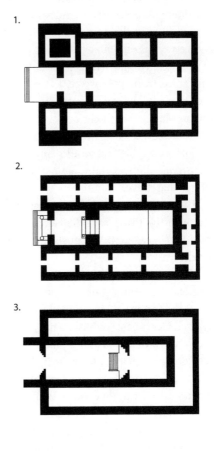

1. Tell Afis, Syria, ninth-eighth century
2. Ain Dara, Syria, ninth-eighth century
3. Solomon's temple footprint

85

Finally, the temple they knew had no doubt been altered considerably over time, so the writers were compelled to extrapolate—and of course to exaggerate. They did the best they could, given the circumstances.

So, there was a real temple in Jerusalem, as elsewhere in the Levant. Solomon's temple was just not quite as grandiose as it seems. And if it was not unique after all, that makes it all the more believable. What made it different was the theological concept and the national sense of identity that it represented. Archaeology can only speculate about such matters.

Among Solomon's other reputed activities is the fortifying of several sites, including Gezer, ceded to him as a dowry by an Egyptian pharaoh whose daughter was presented to Solomon as a wife. Such diplomatic marriages are well attested in the ancient Near East, although an Egyptian pharaoh rarely gives away his daughter (there are a few parallels). The pharaoh (not named, as was the custom then) is undoubtedly Siamun of the Twenty-First Dynasty, who ruled from 978–959 BCE, thus being early in Solomon's reign. The four sites that the biblical narrative in 1 Kings 9:15–17 then names are Jerusalem, Hazor, Megiddo, and Gezer.

All these sites are said to have been built up, or refortified (Hebrew *banah*) by Solomon. This text would appear to provide an ideal opportunity to test the archaeological data against a very clear, undisputed, and well-dated biblical narrative.

The relevant Megiddo gate was excavated in the 1930s, a similar gate at Hazor in the 1950s, and the Gezer gate in the 1960s. No such gate has been found in Jerusalem, because the proper areas have never been available for excavation.

These monumental city gates are unique four-entryway gates, all nearly identical in size and construction. The famed Israeli archaeologist Yigael Yadin excavated the one at Hazor, then re-examined the Megiddo gate and the unrecognized Gezer gate (published in 1912). Something of a military expert himself, Yadin concluded in 1950 that all three gates were so similar that they must have been designed in a single blueprint by architects in some administrative center. But where? Yadin declared: "Jerusalem." And since the pottery dates clustered around the mid-tenth century BCE, Yadin concluded: "Solomonic." The name stuck, but controversies ensued.

Some skeptics, including the biblical revisionists (see Chapter 1), argued that the sensational correlation was simply another example of the bias of old-fashioned biblical archaeology, an attempt to "prove the Bible." But the excavators at Hazor, Gezer, and Megiddo were hardly of that school. One of them (Dever) had long been an outspoken opponent of the older approach.

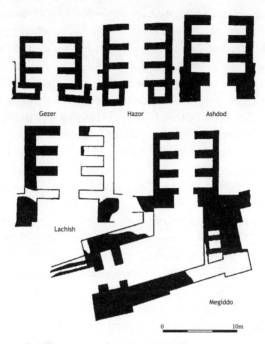

Gezer Hazor Ashdod

Lachish

Megiddo

0   10m

Six-chamber gates of Iron Age Israel

The conclusion was based not on the biblical account of Solomon's vainglory, but rather on the traditional tools of archaeology: pottery chronology, which after a century or more was by now quite accurate; and stratigraphy, or the untangling of successive layers in a mound or buried city.

The relevant Solomonic strata are Gezer VIII, Megiddo VA/IVB, and Hazor X. The evidence from Gezer is particularly well documented. There the city gate in Field III, with at least fourteen superimposed rebuilds, was so violently destroyed that it had to be drastically reconstructed, just after the third street level—that is, perhaps a generation or so after it had been built.

It happens that we have a candidate for the Gezer destruction: the very Pharaoh Shoshenq mentioned above, whose reign corresponds closely with that of Solomon. Since the last century, we have known of an Egyptian royal inscription that lists dozens of sites that this pharaoh is said to have destroyed in a raid ca. 930 BCE. The accompanying scene pictures him as triumphant, holding the more than one hundred captured cities in oval cartouches, like dogs on a leash, each with a place name. Gezer is number twelve, right after Gaza in topographical order.

Biblical scholars are fond of saying that the archaeological record is "mute."

"Show us a text," they say. Here we have a well-dated historical text, and it gives us a fixed date upon which to hang our relative archaeological chronology. If Shoshenq did indeed raid Israel sometime before his death in 924 BCE, that would fall late in Solomon's reign, after several strata levels in the Gezer gate had built up earlier in his reign. So the construction would fall about 950 BCE, midway in his reign. We now have carbon-14 dates that fall precisely then.

Another of Solomon's administrative measures was to divide his realm into twelve administrative districts, each one delegated to supply one month's revenue for his elaborate court. The list is contained in 1 Kings 4:7–19. Skeptics have argued that this list is too late (ca. seventh century BCE) to be reliable. But of the twelve district centers named in the list, ten have been located and excavated. And they all have tenth-century BCE levels that would be relevant. That suggests that the list is based on older, authentic sources and should be taken seriously.

We know that copper was smelted in the Arabah, the dry trough-like southern Jordan valley that separates modern-day Israel and Jordan. From the late fourth millennium BCE onward, the area was known to biblical writers as "Punon," or in Arabic the Wadi Feinan today.

The legend of "King Solomon's lost copper mines" has innumerable worldwide versions and may have begun long ago, perhaps in antiquity. But the Hebrew Bible never mentions his acquiring copper, only gold and silver, and in enormous quantities ("as common as stone"; 2 Chr. 1:15). Nor is Solomon ever associated with sites in the Wadi Arabah where our copper smelters are.

The legend was given new life when the American rabbi-archaeologist Nelson Glueck excavated the presumed site of Ezion-geber near Eilat (Arabic Tell el-Kheleifeh; above) in 1938–1940. Glueck dated the earliest large building to the tenth century BCE and interpreted regularly spaced holes in the mudbrick walls as "flues" for smelting copper. Although Glueck never published a proper excavation report, in his rather flamboyant popular articles he promoted the site as evidence for "King Solomon's copper mines," even claiming the approval of mining engineers. But later reinvestigation of the ruins has shown that the "flues" in the walls are nothing more than recesses for supporting roof-beams. And nothing at the site antedates the eighth or possibly the ninth century BCE. A recent large-scale interdisciplinary project at a number of sites in the Wadi Ifdan region of the Arabah valley in Jordan has revealed an enormous complex of copper-working installations. They were constructed and operated on a truly industrial scale, dating all the way from the fourth millennium BCE to the Roman period and even later. Nothing like this has ever been found anywhere else in the Middle East.

Chronology and Radiocarbon Dating

In archaeology, the traditional tools of chronology were first to use stratigraphy to separate the layers, or strata, in a *tell* or mound, in order to yield a *relative* chronology. Then one would use the evolution in pottery styles to characterize a historical and cultural horizon that might be linked to datable texts, such as a well-documented destruction, which would yield an *absolute* chronology.

In the last few decades the traditional tools of archaeology have been honed to a remarkable degree of accuracy. Nevertheless, a margin of error of a century or so was still common. The great improvement since 1950 has been carbon-14 dating. The element carbon-14 exists in all organisms and remains stable during their lifetime. Then, after death, the carbon-14 slowly dissipates at a constant rate. If one can measure the remaining carbon-14, one can fix the time of death of the organism, yielding a date BP, "before the present."

Beginning around 2000, a vast carbon-14 project was undertaken using samples from dozens of sites and comparing the results from several laboratories. The result is hundreds of published carbon-14 dates, many of which will revolutionize our histories of ancient Israel in all periods.

There is a large fortress with double walls and a three-entryway gate, almost identical to sites well known in Israel. There is also some typical Israelite pottery. A series of adjusted carbon-14 dates begins in the tenth century BCE and possibly even in the late eleventh century BCE. Could this yield evidence of "King Solomon's copper mines"? Caution is needed, as we have learned the hard way. But this really is an eleventh- or tenth-century BCE smelter, with tons of copper slag scattered all around.

Some centralized authority must have been in charge of construction and operation. But who? It cannot have been Egypt, which by now had sunk into a decline in the Third Intermediate period and had lost its Asiatic empire. It is unlikely to have been an Edomite state in southern Jordan (despite the excavators' opinion) since most authorities date Edom's rise as a state to the eighth century BCE at the earliest. No other centralized authority existed in the region in the tenth century BCE except the state of Judah, under Solomon's rule.

If one needs evidence closer to home, other recent excavations in the southern Negev desert in Israel, opposite the Jordanian sites in biblical Judah, have produced similar copper-smelting sites, dated by carbon-14 to the same horizon. And there, extensive copper mines have long been known and are still in operation today.

"Biblical archaeology" or not, it is not unreasonable to suggest that Solomon may indeed have had extensive copper-working facilities. How and where the copper may have been marketed remains unknown. But the seaport at Eilat claimed by the biblical writers would have provided one means of marketing goods.

The rich archaeological data adduced here in support of a biblical "united monarchy" (and there is much more) would be straightforward if it were not for one contentious issue that must now be addressed: chronology.

The archaeological and historical chronology used here is the conventional one, in which the Iron IIA archaeological period is dated to the tenth century BCE, ca. 1000–900 BCE. That accords, of course, precisely with the reigns of Saul, David, and Solomon—the "united monarchy" of biblical scholarship. The term is not used in the Hebrew Bible, but the concept is clearly that "all Israel" is ruled by a single succession of kings, later called the Davidic dynasty. Then the kingdom is divided after Solomon's death into a "divided monarchy," equivalent to our Iron IIB.

The chronological correlations seem sound. But in the mid-1990s, an Israeli archaeologist, Israel Finkelstein, began to advocate for an idiosyncratic "low chronology," which would lower conventional dates by almost a century. His supposed evidence consisted of (1) the fact that Philistine bichrome pottery does not appear at Lachish in the twelfth century BCE, as elsewhere, so that pottery must be later; (2) the pottery conventionally dated to the tenth century BCE could also be dated to the ninth century BCE; (3) radiocarbon dates of various samples turn out to be as much as a century later; (4) the ashlar, chisel-dressed masonry of Samaria must be ninth century BCE, since the Bible shows that the site was founded only in the days of Omri. Consequently, the similar masonry of the gates at Hazor, Megiddo, and Gezer must be down-dated to the ninth century, as with all other related sites.

None of these arguments holds water, even though Finkelstein and his admirers have tirelessly promoted the scheme.

(1) Philistine pottery does not occur at Lachish in the twelfth century BCE simply because the Philistines never penetrated inland that far.

(2) The pottery conventionally dated to the tenth century can indeed continue to the ninth century BCE. We have long known that. But so what? The fact that it can be later does not mean that it must be.

(3) Some relevant radiocarbon dates do fall in the tenth century BCE; but they are few, and many others confirm the conventional "high date." In any case, carbon-14 dates are notoriously difficult to interpret; and even in the best case, they cannot come closer than about fifty years, so they cannot solve the problem themselves.

(4) The appearance of ashlar masonry is no criterion. Such masonry is well attested from the fourteenth century BCE to the Hellenistic era.

Finkelstein's low chronology, never followed by a majority of mainstream scholars, is a house of cards. Yet it is the *only* reason for attributing our copious tenth-century-BCE archaeological evidence of a united monarchy to the ninth century BCE.

Finkelstein himself seems to have doubts. Originally, he insisted that no Judean state emerged until the eighth century BCE. Then it was the ninth century BCE. Eventually he posited a tenth-century-BCE "Saulide polity" with its "hub" at Gibeon—not Jerusalem, and not Solomon, only his predecessor!

But there is absolutely no archaeological evidence for such an imaginary kingdom. Finkelstein's radical scenario is clever, but not convincing. It should be ignored. The reigns of Saul, David, and Solomon are reasonably well attested.

In summing up, what did the kingdom of Saul, David, and Solomon in the tenth century BCE actually look like? First, it was relatively small, about the size of New Jersey. It comprised approximately the area of modern Israel and the West Bank, excluding the Philistine coastal plain south of Tel Aviv and the Phoenician coast north all the way to Haifa and the Lebanon border.

Solomon's rule extending all the way to Tadmor (Palmyra), and even to Mesopotamia (1 Kgs. 4:21–24) is, of course, quite fanciful. Only later would Israel attempt to annex Phoenicia, and even then unsuccessfully. It is doubtful that Israel ever occupied any territory east of the Jordan river; occasional attempted raids are possible but unlikely.

The population had grown, estimates suggesting from around seventy-five thousand in the eleventh century BCE to around one hundred thousand by the tenth century BCE. There was also a decided increase in urbanization and centralization. Many villages were abandoned, towns grew up here and there, and a few cities may have attained a population of up to three thousand. The settlement pattern changed as well. Not only do we find a handful of larger cities, but these are distributed in a pattern so that each seems to have managed its own larger surrounding territory. Archaeologists describe such an arrangement in terms of "central place theory." That looks like Solomon's attempt to reorganize the country. Thus some people lived in urban centers, but the vast majority remained rural.

Jerusalem, however, while certainly built up, remained largely occupied by those administrative classes that were attached to the crown, as well as by a large clerical establishment. What we know of Jerusalem in the tenth century suggests such a situation.

Israel was to some degree isolated in this period, moving somewhat hesitatingly from "tribe to nation" as it were. Israel had by now a distinct sense of peoplehood, but little concept of national destiny. The integrated picture of this fully developed state—"all Israel" —is a later literary concept, projected by the biblical writers back onto earlier days.

Israel's neighbors in the tenth century were all known to the biblical writers: Philistines, Phoenicians, Arameans, and the peoples of Transjordan. We can now characterize all of them on the basis of current archaeological evidence, especially the Philistines. But again, the biblical writers describe these people largely on the basis of what they knew of them in their own day.

In any case, early Israel by the tenth century BCE does look like a state or kingdom by the overall criteria. It boasts a king, a capital, a centralized administration, in all probability a small standing army, a well-established economy and some industry (pottery), a reasonably well-developed sense of ethnic identity, a national language (classical Hebrew), and the beginnings of literacy. The latter is particularly significant. We have already noted that at the small remote fort of Qeiyafa someone was able to use an offshoot of the old Canaanite alphabet well enough to have kept simple administrative economic transactions and records. One other inscription of the tenth century BCE, in a similar script, was found at Tell Zayit. It gives the letters of the alphabet in what is becoming a Hebrew script. It is thus a practice text. Even in a small Judean village a few people are learning to write, perhaps not just professional scribes.

We actually have a tenth-century schoolboy's practice text, a clay tablet found at Gezer. It is a calendar, giving the planting seasons of the agricultural year—a mnemonic poem like "thirty days hath September." The fact that people are learning to write in their own script and language means that the idea of some biblical sources going back to the early days of the monarchy is not inherently fantastic.

What Is Left and Does It Matter?

Again we shall use our revised history of the rise of the state, based on newer archaeological data, to inquire what ordinary people—not those who wrote the Bible—may have experienced in the tenth century.

First, most people were still village farmers. Even though others were attracted to the supposed advantages of urban life and were gravitating to a few growing cities, they would have upheld the values of rural life.

The Philistines—who we must remember were essentially Europeans, Aegean invaders—were now encroaching on the Israelite heartland in the hill country. So out of fear for their very lives, always precarious, many people would have gone along reluctantly with the growing demand for a king to lead them. This is what elites like Samuel and others, as well as some city folk, insisted was their only alternative.

Soon there was a capital city, and kings, and conscriptions, and what seemed like continuing wars and taxes. Rumors had it that there was a magnificent temple in Jerusalem, run by an official priestly class. And there was now an elite establishment of bureaucrats, career military, merchants, entrepreneurs, and other urbanites.

For the majority of Israelites, however, with at least ninety percent of the population living in the rural areas, all this was new and disconcerting. It was said that there were professional scribes in Jerusalem who were beginning to write a history of the new "Israel"; but it was not their Israel.

The archaeology-based history of the tenth century presented here obviously reflects the above lifestyle. It also fits extraordinarily well with the picture of the deep-seated ambivalence toward kingship in one strand of the tradition preserved in the books of Samuel.

It is instructive that the final editors of the Hebrew Bible incorporated in the books of Samuel *both* the polemics for and against the institution of kingship. That was a genuine and realistic reflection of the widespread uncertainties of life in an evolving national state and its cult. Archaeology does not challenge that portrait; it confirms it. That was the way it really was in the tenth century BCE.

We have rewritten the story of the early monarchy in Israel in the light of the archaeological evidence, making the heroes a bit "smaller than life," the events a bit less grandiose. That does not mean, of course, that the moral value of the stories is necessarily diminished, if we read critically, as we have done previously.

The first lesson is that the development of statehood is neither an inevitable stage of cultural evolution, nor always a sign of progress. There are advanced civilizations, like that of the Han dynasty in China, that never achieved true statehood. In theory, early Israel might have continued indefinitely as a society without a sovereign. Yahweh was Israel's sovereign, as Samuel reminded enthusiasts. It may indeed have been the Philistine crises that triggered the rise of the state, as again the Bible maintains. Otherwise, who knows?

A state may best be considered as a necessary evil. It has its attractions, and it may seem the only alternative to internal chaos and external threats. Politics is all about power. But power corrupts; and centralized power, in the hands of the few, can lead to an oppressive authoritarian form of government—as indeed Israel became under later kings.

The early monarchy was a social and political experiment. It required a trade-off, just as Samuel had warned. The king may secure your borders, but your sons will pay for that. That this risk continued to be well understood by later Israelites is attested by perennial rebellions against the monarchy (and institutionalized religion), especially in the north, despite the biblical writers regarding all this as sanctioned by Yahweh. Thus, as we have seen, the prophetic cry from time to time: "To your tents, O Israel!" That, however, was more nostalgia than an effective program for reform. The Israelite state was there to stay. And David, despite all his flaws, remained the ideal king, "God's anointed."

A further lesson is that kings, however legitimated, are not above the law; they must be held accountable to the people, and above all to God and to natural law. All totalitarian forms of government must be resisted and if possible overthrown. An irrefutable principle is that all are equal under the law. Prophets and social reformers may be needed to call us to reform, but a theocracy is unacceptable. A final lesson from the early monarchy is that larger-than-life heroes may make great stories. But great men and their public deeds do not necessarily make for the best history. All three of the early kings of Israel embody a more existentially tragic sense of history, in the Greek sense of "tragedy," when bad things happen to good people.

Saul is a man of great natural gifts; but he is overwhelmed by the daunting conditions he faces, and he sinks into depression and madness, dying apparently at an early age. David is even more of a contradiction: attractive, outrageous, and often self-destructive, but beloved by the common folk. After a victory against the Philistines, the young David dances naked through the streets of Jerusalem, and the women sing his praises. Today, a David would be locked up.

Even Solomon, the poster-boy, ends up with a lavish display of wealth at the people's expense—an example of wretched excess. And while he may not have had a thousand wives, he did have too many.

Whatever the case, the Israelite state was there to stay. The Davidic line of kings would remain on the throne in Judah for four hundred years. The north, though, was perennially unstable, as we shall see.

CHAPTER 6

Israel, a Nation among the Nations: Divine Destiny—and Disaster

The Biblical Narrative

In covering what we call the divided monarchy during the Iron II period in the ninth to sixth centuries BCE, we face a different challenge in integrating text and artifact. Heretofore the archaeological data seemed to question the biblical narratives, so that some interpretive sleight-of-hand was required to defend our rather minimalistic rewrite of biblical history. Now, however, the archaeological data comprise more of an additional *commentary*, usually supplementing the biblical narratives in very positive ways. That is because the accounts in the books of 1 and 2 Kings are concerned largely with *political* history and take little notice of anything else. And archaeology can do political history quite well.

The books of 1 and 2 Kings cover the history of a divided monarchy over a period of a little more than three hundred years (920–586 BCE). Over the course of these years, Judah saw nineteen kings, all of the Davidic line, while the breakaway kingdom of northern Israel, enduring for a shorter span of history (down to ca. 722 BCE), saw a total of nine kings. In contrast to the elaborate coverage given to David, the account of a monarch's reign is now often reduced to a brief formulaic notice: "Y succeeded his father X; reigned . . . years; did evil in the sight of Yahweh; and died and was buried with his fathers." These are more snapshots than fully fleshed-out portraits.

For instance, the reign of Omri, the founder of the most important dynasty in the north, is covered in only twelve verses (1 Kgs. 16:17–28). From these few verses in Kings, we learn only: (1) that Omri was a renegade who supplanted Tibni, supported by a popular uprising; (2) that after six years he moved the

The Divided Monarchy

capital from Tirzah to Samaria, where he ruled for six more years; (3) that he did evil in the eyes of Yahweh; and (4) that he died and was replaced by his son Ahab.

The curt account in the Bible must be compared with extrabiblical texts to see if there is any biblical motivation for minimizing Omri, the enemy of Judah. The Neo-Assyrian annals regard Omri as so significant that for more than one hundred years after his rule they designate the northern kingdom of Israel as *Bīt-Ḫumria,* "the dynasty [literally 'house'] of Omri." Today we could easily write a whole volume on the Omri-Ahab dynasty on the basis of the archaeological remains: its magnificent capital at Samaria, the palace and its luxurious furnishings, Phoenician relations, ostraca (texts written on potsherds) detailing socioeconomic conditions, and foreign wars. Which is the better source for the historian interested not in theological judgments, but focused on a larger history of events? Clearly the archaeological data are "primary"—more abundant, more varied, more contemporary and trustworthy.

First let us look at the major historical events of the divided monarchy. For our purposes, we will separate our discussion between the north and the south, despite the biblical writers' and editors' deliberate mingling of them together so as to preserve the old notion of "all Israel." It must be remembered that the text of the books of Kings as we have it was largely written by Judeans and reflects their "royal (or Davidic) theology." But none of the northern kings were from the Davidic line, so the writers are critical of every single king in the north. They *all* "did evil in the sight of Yahweh." Surely not.

All the kings of Israel and Judah, together with their approximate dates, may be listed in chart form. Those known also from extrabiblical texts are designated by an asterisk.

Rulers of United and Divided Monarchies

Saul

Ishbaal (2 years)

David 1010–970

Solomon 970–931/930

Kingdom of Judah		Kingdom of Israel	
Rehoboam	931/930–915/914	Jeroboam	931/930–911/910
Abijam	915/914–912/911	Nadab	911/910
Asa	912/911–871/870	Baasha	910/909–887/886
		Elah	887/886–886/885
		Zimri	7 days
		Tibni	5 years (rival to Omri)
		Omri	886/885–875/874
Jehoshaphat	871/870–849/848	Ahab	875/874–853
J(eh)oram	849/848–842	Ahaziah	853–852
Ahaziah	842–841	J(eh)oram	852–841
Athaliah (queen)	841–835	Jehu	841–814/813
Joash	841/835–796/795	Jehoahaz	814/813–806/805
Amaziah	796/795–767/766	Jehoash	806/805–791/790
Uzziah (Azariah)	783–732	Jeroboam II	791/790–750/749
Jotham	750–735/734	Zechariah	750/749
		Shallum	1 month
		Menahem	749/748–739/738

		Pekahiah	738–737/736
Ahaz	735/734–715	Pekah	737/736–732/731
Hezekiah	715–687	Hoshea	732/731–722
Manasseh	697–642		
Amon	642–640		
Josiah	640–609		
Jehoahaz	3 months		
Jehoiakim	609–598		
Jehoiachin	598/597		
Zedekiah	597–586		

The North

Here we can summarize only the most significant events, limiting ourselves to three or four of the most outstanding kings. We have already noted the terse account of Omri's reign in the books of Kings. His son, Ahab, is given much more space.

Ahab is declared at once to have been even worse than his father, because he actively promoted the worship of Baal—the old Canaanite storm god—right in the capital of Samaria. He even married a Phoenician princess, the wicked Jezebel from Sidon. Among Ahab's unjust actions that the prophets condemn is building a "house of ivory" at Samaria. This was an enigmatic reference until fairly recently, but no doubt an example of conspicuous consumption. Ahab is credited, however, with founding many apparently new cities. All these and other deeds are said to have been recorded in the *Book of the Chronicles of the Kings of Israel,* a document lost to us.

The first of the major prophets, Elijah, is now introduced to condemn the apostasy. An account of the famous contest between Yahweh and Baal on Mount Carmel follows. Elijah and Yahweh carry the day, and Elijah is commanded to anoint Hazael as king of Damascus in Syria (as though he were able to do so). Then he is to anoint one Jehu, a general in the army who is famed for his breakneck chariot driving, as a claimant to the throne.

Not surprisingly, Ben-hadad, king of Syria, forms a coalition of thirty-two fellow Aramean city-state kings. They besiege Samaria and demand tribute. But Ahab surprises them in their camp and slaughters all but Ben-hadad, who escapes. Elijah is not impressed and warns Ahab that within the year the Arameans will return. They do return, but Ahab kills one hundred thousand of their troops. Nevertheless, a treaty is signed, allowing the Arameans to have mutually accepted merchants and shops in both countries.

Ahab, at Jezebel's insistence, confiscates the vineyard of one Naboth at Jezreel, near Samaria, conniving to have him executed as a criminal. After three years of peace, a war with Judah breaks out. But both sides soon collaborate in order to face a threat from Syria once more.

They meet the king of Syria at Ramoth-gilead in northern Transjordan, but Ahab is recognized and killed. When his retainers bring his chariot and his body back to Samaria, the dogs lick up his blood in the streets (as they soon will Jezebel's).

Ahab's son Jehoram now takes the throne. Having learned nothing from his father's fate, he mounts a campaign at Ramoth-gilead against a new Aramean king, Hazael, accompanied by his ally, Ahaziah king of Judah. Jehoram is wounded, and he and Ahaziah retreat to Jezreel to recover. Their army deserts to Jehu, an opportunist who rushes to Jezreel and kills both kings. He has been incited to violence all along by the prophet Elijah.

Ahab's seventy sons and his queen Jezebel are all executed. Jezebel's body is thrown from a window in the palace down to the streets where dogs consume it. Jehu, although he is a usurper who ascended the throne in a bloody coup, rules then for twenty-seven years. In his favor, he is said to have purged the northern kingdom of the cult of Baal. But another passage in Kings declares that he actually expanded the influence by setting up golden calves at the old cult sites of Bethel and Dan, that is, pagan shrines at the northern and southern borders.

Only thirty-five years after Jehu's death Jeroboam II takes the throne. He rules for thirty-nine years (forty-one in the Bible), longer than any other northern king. But the book of 2 Kings allots him only eight verses, again denouncing him as evil like his predecessors. Nevertheless, it reluctantly credits him with restoring territory down to the coastal plain and even taking Damascus. Obviously a great many details of political history at this juncture have been omitted from the biblical account. That may be because there was now an interval when campaigns by a new enemy, Assyria, were infrequent. Thus Israel enjoyed a rare respite from international intrigue and a period of relative stability and prosperity.

Little that is deemed noteworthy follows during accounts of the brief reigns of several successive kings in the north (some only a year or two long). Then we come to the reign of Hoshea, the last king of the north, who ruled from 732 to 722 BCE.

Events of this era led to the utter destruction and the end of the northern kingdom of Israel. Yet the southern writers relate these momentous events in a mere seven verses (2 Kgs. 15:29; 17:3–6, 23, 24). This diminishment reflects the rival biblical writers' and editors' nationalist, pro-Yahwistic bias. In their view, the apostates in the north got what they deserved. Their destruction was justified by the fact that they had violated the covenant with Moses.

The only historical details in the brief accounts in Kings comprise the mention that Samaria was besieged for three years and captured by the Assyrian king Shalmaneser V, and that the captives were carried into exile in Assyria, to Halah on the Habor River and to Media.

In another passage, Tiglath-pileser III is said to be the victor (2 Kgs. 15:29). The few sites he destroyed include Ijon, Abel-beth-maacah on the northern border, Janoah, Kedesh, Hazor, Gilead, Galilee, and "all the land of Naphtali." He too deports the captives to Assyria. That is absolutely *all* the biblical narratives put together deign to tell us.

The South

In Judah, Solomon's son Rehoboam inherits the now divided kingdom. It will still be called "Israel" because it, and it alone, is the legitimate state, the true "people of Yahweh." Rehoboam is said to have ruled over Judah for seventeen years. Yet little is said of any events except to revile him for allowing his queen mother Maacah to "make an abominable image of Asherah," and he himself allows the high places to continue. His heart is not perfect, but Yahweh spares him "for David's sake."

Rehoboam's grandson, Asa, confronts Baasha, his rival king in the north, but is unsuccessful. The Jerusalem temple is looted, and all Rehoboam's heirs are executed. Ben-hadad, the Aramean king, was purportedly in league with Asa, but to no avail.

The next important king in Judah, some sixty years after Ahaziah is killed by Jehu, is Uzziah (also named Azariah). He is said to have ruled for fifty-two years, during which many events took place, including above all the Assyrian onslaught and destruction of the northern kingdom in 732–722 BCE. Yet the account in Kings recounts Uzziah's reign in only seven verses, no doubt because he, like his forefathers, did not destroy the high places. For that failing, Yahweh struck him with leprosy.

We turn now to one of only two kings of whom the southern writers of the Bible approve—Hezekiah the reformer. He is on the throne when the Assyrians conquer Samaria, but he rebels and gets away with it. Judah is spared for another twenty years until the Assyrians return and renew their campaigns into the Levant under Sennacherib. The Assyrians themselves are soon to be overrun by the Babylonians.

The campaign of Sennacherib to Judah in 701 BCE is one of the best documented of such campaigns in the history of the ancient Near East. The books of Kings supplement the Neo-Assyrian annals and the archaeological record (below) well, devoting two long chapters to it (2 Kgs. 18–19). In the Assyrian account of the campaign, Sennacherib boasts of having destroyed forty-six Judean towns, and then shutting up Hezekiah "like a bird in a cage." Presumably the siege is successful.

The biblical account, however, mentions Sennacherib only once or twice, noting merely that he was at Lachish and Libnah, the former being the greatest fortress in all Judah after Jerusalem. Then 2 Kings relates an elaborate story of the miraculous deliverance of Jerusalem and the Temple of Yahweh. It is said that 185,000 Assyrian soldiers were killed by an angel of Yahweh, whereupon Sennacherib returned to Nineveh and was later assassinated by two of his sons. The stark and ironic contrasts between the two accounts will be explored later.

Hezekiah is depicted victoriously first and foremost because he is said to have been a strict Yahwist. He "trusted in Yahweh" and kept all his commandments, unlike almost all of the other kings. He destroyed all the pagan sanctuaries, north and south. Moreover, he prudently foresaw that the Assyrians would regroup after their campaigns in the north. So he prepared for a siege by securing Jerusalem's water supply—never very reliable—directing the water of the Gihon spring to a reservoir within the city walls by means of a conduit (2 Kgs. 20:20).

The only other southern king to be discussed here is another reformer, Josiah, who reigned from 640–609 BCE during the final years of Judah. Like Hezekiah some eighty years before, he is blessed by Yahweh—even more so, because he "walked in all the ways of his father David." Furthermore, he repairs the temple, which had been plundered during the siege.

Hilkiah the high priest and Shaphan the scribe come to Josiah, declaring that they have discovered a supposedly long-lost scroll, the "book of the Law," in the course of the temple renovations. Most scholars think that this was in fact a version of what we know as the book of Deuteronomy, essentially the basic laws of Moses. This document was probably not "lost" at all, but was brought to the king and the people by prophetic reformers and orthodox priests in order to serve as the blueprint for sweeping religious reforms. Judah must repent, or else be lost like Samaria.

Just such reforms are described in 2 Kings 23, which enumerates in detail a number of specific actions Josiah is said to have taken. The list is certainly comprehensive. But were any such reforms ever successfully carried out? We shall return to that question below.

Within a few years, the heroic king Josiah meets his end when in 609 BCE

Deuteronomy and the Deuteronomistic History

There is a curious story in 2 Kings 22 about how Josiah's reforms in the late seventh century BCE were promoted by the discovery of a lost scroll in the temple while it was being renovated. The scroll was sent to the king by Hilkiah the high priest, and when the king heard the "book of the Law" read to him, he tore his clothes in despair. The king then convened all the leaders of Judah and demanded that the population renew its covenant with Moses. The narrative then relays a famous list of the people's apostasies (2 Kgs. 23:4–14)—even in the temple in Jerusalem—and how good King Josiah restored "authentic" monotheistic religion.

Most biblical scholars now believe that discovered scroll was a version of the present book of Deuteronomy (the name meaning significantly "Second Law"), which was then added to the rest of the Pentateuch to complete it as a five-scroll work attributed to Moses. More important, it was used as a prolegomenon to the extant works that form the great epic of Israel's history from Sinai to the fall of Jerusalem in 586 BCE. It is this great composite work—including Joshua, Judges, 1–2 Samuel, and 1–2 Kings—compiled toward the end of Israel's history that scholars call the Deuteronomistic History.

he attempts to intercept an Egyptian column moving north, probably to aid the Assyrian forces. But he is killed at Megiddo, his body is brought back to Jerusalem, and he is buried there. He is much mourned, but the end of the Judean monarchy has not yet arrived.

From Josiah's death in 609 BCE to the fall of Jerusalem in 586 BCE there were four hapless kings, two of them surviving only a year or two each. The account of how the Babylonian king Nebuchadnezzar besieged and destroyed Jerusalem in two raids extends through 2 Kings 24–25. First, in 597 BCE, Nebuchadnezzar deports Jehoiachin, who had ruled only three months as a puppet of Babylon, together with all the royal family. All the ruling elites, the militia, the craftsmen, and other professionals are deported, leaving only those characterized as "the people of the land," possibly the lower classes and the rural population. The Babylonians then install Zedekiah as king in Jerusalem.

In 586 BCE Nebuchadnezzar returns. He besieges Jerusalem for a short period of time, destroys the temple and all its furnishings, burns all the nobles' houses, and razes the city walls to the ground. Poor Zedekiah is dragged off to Riblah in Syria, where he is blinded after being forced to watch the execution of his sons. Then Zedekiah is carried off to Babylon and enslaved.

The account in Kings, the whole chronicle of the monarchy, north and south, ends with the notice that Evil-merodach, a successor of Nebuchadnezzar, allows Jehoiachin, who had been exiled earlier to Babylon, to eat at his table—that is, to scramble for crumbs on the floor, a common way of humiliating high-ranking captives.

Looking at the conclusion of 2 Kings, two things are significant. First, no site other than Jerusalem is mentioned at all in the text, despite the fact that the whole of the Judean kingdom was devastated, never to recover. Only the loss of Jerusalem and the temple is mourned. They were the visible symbols of Yahweh's covenant with his people Israel and of his promise to David that his house would rule forever.

Second, with these cataclysmic events, the six-hundred-year history of Israel and Judah comes to an end. There is nothing more to chronicle in the Hebrew Bible. It is all over, due to Israel's feckless behavior, its "whoring after other gods." What is more striking is that now, with the sweeping epic from Sinai to Babylon having come to a disastrous end, Yahweh simply *disappears*. As the Bible says in more than one place, Yahweh declares, "I will hide my face from them. I shall see what their end will be" (Deut. 31:17, 18, among other places). Now the Israelites are on their own.

In the remainder of the Hebrew Bible, covering the exile and a modest return to Jerusalem, Yahweh is scarcely again seen or heard. His word, spoken through the earlier prophets, falls silent. Richard Elliott Friedman documents all this in his illuminating book, *The Disappearance of God*. Friedman says of this:

> The more we know about the people who wrote and edited the Bible, the *harder* it is to explain how it came out with such consistent developments as the hiding of the face of God and the shift in the divine-human balance. How could this have happened?[1]

All that is left of ancient Israel and Judah is a far-distant hope: the Messiah. Judaism is still waiting.

An Archaeological Critique

Here our task is somewhat simpler, perhaps more reassuring, than it has been thus far. For the entire three-hundred-year history of the divided monarchy the archaeological evidence contradicts the biblical stories in some

---

1. Richard Elliott Friedman, *The Disappearance of God: A Divine Mystery* (Boston: Little, Brown & Company), 86.

significant ways. But more often than not, it tends to undergird the biblical account, sometimes in striking detail. What archaeology does do particularly and uniquely well, however, is to fill in many gaps left by the biblical record, especially about matters other than politics, such as the lives of the ordinary people.

The books of Kings, not surprisingly, are all about kings and the great public events of their reigns—politics and international intrigue—occasionally mentioning religion only when it is deemed to be relevant. There is very little notice of anything else. Of the dozens and dozens of Israelite sites that we now know, many of them excavated, only a few are even mentioned. Even the realm's administrative centers are largely passed over. There are few hints of population growth; of distinctive features of the economy and society; of art, architecture, and aesthetics; of popular folk religion (except to excoriate it); of burials; of literacy; or even of growing national ethnic confidence.

One striking omission in 2 Kings is that the major prophet Isaiah, who lived during the reigns of several kings, is mentioned only several times during the crisis in Hezekiah's day. And the other prophets of the time, Amos, Hosea, and Micah—all important public figures—are not mentioned at all. We know the latter only through the books bearing their names. Yet the *context* of their work, which so enhances the meaning of their prophecies, should surely have been covered by Kings if this is really history. Is this simply a southern bias?

Most deafening is the silence concerning the lives of ordinary people, the masses who after all help to make history. Do they count for nothing? To that we shall return shortly.

The North

Let us look first at the northern kingdom, which, although by now estranged from the south, is called "Israel." We have already noted the Bible's terse dismissal of the heretic Omri, even though the Assyrian annals reveal that he was recalled for a century or more as a great king of Israel. Omri's first capital at Tirzah has been identified as Tell el-Far'ah, a prominent site at the head of a major valley leading up from the Jordan valley to the central hills. Excavations by French archaeologists have revealed a flourishing ninth-century city that shows signs of unfinished or altered houses and a city gate that seems to have changed. That may illuminate Omri's change of venue to Samaria.

Samaria was excavated by British and Israeli archaeologists in the 1930s. Today we could easily write a whole volume on Omri's (and Ahab's) splendid capital at Samaria—its elaborate Phoenician-style furnishings, the palace, its luxurious furnishings, the multicultural religious situation, and the written archives that document social and economic conditions in the north. Finely carved ivory plaques imported from Phoenicia and used to inlay furniture were discovered in the palace at Samaria. Now we understand the prophets who condemned the conspicuous consumption of the rich—those who live in "houses of ivory" and lie on "beds of ivory" (1 Kgs. 22:39; Ps. 45:8; Amos 3:15; 6:4). Here a broader history based on nonbiblical data leads to new interpretations and is also morally edifying.

When the Assyrian king Shalmaneser III met a coalition of a dozen or so petty kings in the west, at the battle of Qarqar in Syria in 853 BCE, Omri's son Ahab is listed among these kings. He is credited with having had ten thousand soldiers and two thousand chariots, more than any other king save one. Compare that with the fact that the Bible doesn't even mention this pivotal event, and it characterizes Ahab almost entirely negatively. Here the independent witness of the extrabiblical texts (brought to light by archaeology, having been dug up) is particularly illuminating.

Ahab is credited in the Bible with building many cities (1 Kgs. 22:39) that are said to be mentioned in the lost "chronicles" of the kings of Israel. Although nothing more is said of such cities, the brief notice is correct. We know of at least seventy-five ninth-century BCE cities, and several dozen have been excavated. They show without doubt that by the ninth century BCE, urban development had accelerated, especially in the north, and it had brought much greater stability and prosperity. Ahab's achievements can thus be corroborated and expanded.

Most of these cities, whether new establishments or augmented older towns, were by now heavily fortified with city walls and multiple-entryway gates. Examples would be Dan, Hazor, Jezreel, Megiddo, Tirzah, Shechem, and of course the capital Samaria. Here, too, the archaeological evidence helps to put Israel's growing international role and prominence into a better perspective.

Ahab is said to have perceived the growing threat of the neighboring Aramean city-states in Syria. So he developed a policy of dealing with the Aramean king, Ben-hadad of Damascus, as an equal. First he had to face Ben-hadad and his forces, but instead of paying tribute he defeated them (1 Kgs. 20). Later, as we know from the Assyrian annals, Ahab negotiated a treaty with Hadadezer of Damascus in order to prepare for an Assyrian advance westward.

We happen to know a lot about Arameans at this juncture: they did pose a significant threat to Ahab and his successors from about 880 to ca. 810 BCE. And we have in extrabiblical sources the names of Ben-hadad and Hadadezer of Damascus, who had led the coalition against Shalmaneser III (discussed above). We even have a royal inscription of Ben-hadad. But the biblical accounts in 1 Kings 20 and 22 cannot be reconciled with the Aramean and Assyrian records that we have. The biblical writers seem to have arbitrarily synchronized several different sources that they had at their disposal.

In conclusion, the biblical writers knew something about the general era of the Aramean wars, and they even had some details. And there is also clear archaeological evidence of Aramean invasions well into Judah in the mid- to late ninth century BCE. Excavations at Dan, Hazor, and other northern sites show destruction levels and rebuilds. Rehov, on the west coast of the Sea of Galilee, in the ninth century BCE has predominantly Aramean material culture, as do other sites like Tel Hadar and Bethsaida around the other shores. Even Philistia was affected. At Gath, defenders against an Aramean attack dug an enormous ditch and counter-ramp all around the site, which excavators date to this horizon.

There are other problems in correlating the biblical story of Ahab with the archaeological data. Ahab is said to have ruled Moab in Transjordan (2 Kgs. 3:4-5), as David, Solomon, and Omri were also said to have done. And we even have a well-preserved royal inscription of Mesha, the king of Moab, found in the mid-ninth century at his capital Dibon. It mentions both Omri and Ahab, claiming that the Moabite deity Chemosh had delivered Moab from Israelite rule. That would seem to fit well with 2 Kings 3:5, which mentions in passing that Mesha, king of Moab, had rebelled against Israel after Ahab's death.

Dibon (modern Dhiban), south of Amman, has been excavated. But it shows little or no evidence of a palace fit for a king in the ninth century BCE. And elsewhere in Moab (and Ammon as well), extensive excavated evidence shows no real Israelite material culture. There may well have been some ethnic Israelites living in Transjordan, but a large occupying force would almost certainly have left traces in the archaeological record, as the Arameans did in Israel. Most authorities see Ammon, Moab, and Edom as developing their own independent cultures at this time. The material culture, and the languages as well, show a close relationship with Israel, not military clashes. In any case, the Mesha stele may have been largely royal propaganda, like most other similar inscriptions here. A claim to have been occupied by a foreign power would have provided an ideal opportunity for a Moabite king to aggrandize himself.

One final possible convergence of our two sources is more positive. As we saw above, Ahab conspired to seize Naboth's vineyard and establish what was no doubt a winter palace for himself at Jezreel, on the border of the warmer climate in the Jezreel valley some twenty miles distant. Excavations there in the 1990s by Israeli archaeologists have brought to light a unique walled compound built with royal masonry. It is dated securely to the mid-ninth century BCE, and it was constructed mostly on levels previously only sparsely occupied. After a brief period, the fort came to an end. There can be no doubt that this is Ahab's palace, abandoned sometime after his unfortunate demise.

It was Jehu who, according to the Bible, assassinated Ahab and his family in the military coup discussed above. We have noted that the Aramean victory stele found at Dan claims instead that it was the Aramean king, probably Hazael of Damascus, who credits himself with killing both the Israelite and the Judean kings. Here we have a conflict that we cannot resolve. Both accounts seem believable; and in the nature of the case archaeology cannot decide.

The Aramean king Hazael is mentioned in 2 Kings 13:3, 25 as having repeatedly defeated Israel in battle during the reign of Jehoahaz, who ruled from 814 to 806 BCE. The dates fit for the latter part of Hazael's reign, when Aram was one of the most powerful entities in the area. And the successful raids of the Arameans into both Israel and Judah have been noted above. Here the biblical writers may have gotten it right.

Now we skip some eighty years forward, to the end of the northern kingdom of Israel as a result of Assyrian invasions in 732–722 BCE. The biblical account in 2 Kings 15:19–17:24 describes the context of these campaigns in some detail, but mostly with reference to Samaria. The only other sites mentioned are Ijon (in the Iyyon valley on the southern border of Lebanon); Abel-beth-maacah, a gateway into northern Israel; Janoah; Kedesh, also on the border; and Hazor to the south, but guarding the main north-south highway. Then three general districts are named: Gilead, Galilee, and "all the land of Naphtali."

We happen to have, in addition, Assyrian texts that also mention "Abilakka" and "the wide land of Naphtali." Here the biblical and the Assyrian records are in striking agreement, so the biblical writers have given us a specific, credible account. Nevertheless, only five sites are identified as having been destroyed, although the biblical record is clear that the whole of the northern kingdom was utterly devastated in the Assyrian campaigns.

The writers' main concern was of course Samaria, the capital. The excavations there do give evidence of major disturbances (below). Abel-beth-maacah is being excavated, and there are indications of a destruction. Janoah has apparently been located, but it has not been excavated. Kedesh is a prominent mound right on the northern border, but excavations thus far are not helpful. The three named regions are not detailed enough to allow any reconstruction.

To highlight the differing accounts and reconstruct the actual historical situations, we must observe that today we know of at least a dozen Israelite sites that have been excavated and exhibit major destruction layers that date to this period. Here the additional information that archaeology supplies is not merely interesting, it is crucial for understanding what the actual events were that brought an end to the northern kingdom. The Assyrian relocation of the peoples of the northern kingdom of Israel is the origin of the myth of "the ten lost tribes of Israel"—more than a myth.

One site destroyed by the Assyrians, though not mentioned in the Bible, is Gezer, which was on the border with Judah. There the Assyrian destruction is horrifyingly clear. The lower city wall near the gate was breached, hastily shored up, then destroyed. The upper double city wall was burned, the fiery destruction yielding heavily burnt and calcified pottery and iron arrowheads. Gezer is uniquely represented in an apparent "eyewitness" battlefield sketch. It is an Assyrian cuneiform tablet found long ago in Iraq showing an Assyrian onslaught with a battering ram against a gate tower and reading the "siege of Gezer."

At Samaria the archaeological evidence is difficult to reconcile with the biblical text. According to 2 Kings the site was besieged for three years under Shalmaneser V and destroyed. Then captives were deported to Assyria, and new peoples were brought in to replace them. The account in 2 Kings 17:3; 18:9 is fairly detailed, but there are problems.

One problem is easily solved. The biblical account names Shalmaneser as the conqueror, whereas the Assyrian account specifies that it was Sargon. As it turns out, both versions are correct. It was indeed Shalmaneser who laid the three-year siege (probably more like one and a half years). But he died in the interval, and it was his successor Sargon II who actually conquered the city, claiming to have deported 27,900 captives (more likely from the whole region, if true). But even here there are difficulties.

The famous British archaeologist Kathleen Kenyon had helped to excavate the mound of Samaria in the 1930s. She claimed to have discovered a late eighth-century-BCE heavy destruction layer all around the site, followed by evidence of a hiatus in occupation. But more recent analysis of the site has concluded that at Samaria a "direct correspondence between archaeological history and political history does not always exist."[2] There is a disturbance, and afterward an Assyrian garrison is established at the site. The district of

2. Ron E. Tappy, *The Archaeology of Israelite Samaria*, vol. 2: *The Eighth Century BCE*, Harvard Semitic Studies 50 (Leiden: Brill, 2001), 441.

Samaria and the whole of the northern kingdom did pass into Assyrian hands, but the Bible's exaggerated depiction of the utter annihilation of Samaria is evidently due to the writers' sense of revenge. Samaria is destroyed because Israel has sinned against Yahweh and thus *deserves* to be punished—precisely as the prophets had warned (see 2 Kgs. 17:6–18). The northerners got what they deserved. Happily, Judah was spared.

The South

The history of the southern kingdom of Judah during the divided monarchy as recorded in the Hebrew Bible could be regarded as more accurate and reliable, since the southern writers were closer to the facts and also less biased.

The first king of Judah after the schism was Rehoboam (930–914), Solomon's son. As one of his accomplishments according to Chronicles (but not Kings, which is likely more authoritative), Rehoboam consolidated his newly isolated kingdom by building up several defense cities, among them Lachish (2 Chr. 11:9). Several excavations there have shown that the city was destroyed in the twelfth century BCE and was deserted for a considerable time thereafter. The occupation resumed in either the late tenth century or the early ninth century BCE, when a large citadel, Palace A, was constructed, and possibly a city wall. Some archaeologists have argued that these obvious attempts at building up the site of Lachish represent the work of Rehoboam, as the Bible claims in Chronicles. The dates of his reign, ca. 930–914, would coincide if these events occurred, as we would expect, early in Rehoboam's reign.

Of the other fourteen cities mentioned in the biblical text, only Beth-zur has been extensively excavated, and it appears to be deserted in this period.

For the next 150 years or so, the history of Judah as narrated in the Bible is difficult to correlate with our archaeological evidence, even though the latter is abundant. The authors and editors of the Bible are preoccupied with their polemics against the Judean kings, all of whom are condemned except Hezekiah and Josiah.

Jehoshaphat (870–848) is said to have attempted to seize Ramoth-gilead in Transjordan, in league with Ahab, but that seems unlikely. Then he confronts the "king of Syria," who would be Hazael, a historical note that may have some credence. But Hazael was entrenched in Transjordan and would not have been threatened by the Judean king.

Jehoram (848–842) rules briefly, apparently overlapping with Jehoshaphat, and he is said to have put down a revolt at Elath on the Red Sea (modern Eilat). The port could be either Ezion-geber or the offshore island of Jezirat Farun

(Coral Island). The former has been excavated and mistakenly associated with King Solomon's copper mines (see above). But there was a large walled fort with a four-entryway gate like others that date to this general era. Nothing more can be said. Jezirat Farun has not been excavated.

Ahaziah (841) was the hapless Judean king killed in the Jehu revolt discussed above. He is thus attested in the Tel Dan stele, an authentic character but insignificant.

Athaliah (841–835) is distinguished by being the only female ruler in ancient Israel and Judah. There are no archaeological data on her reign, however, and she rules only in tandem with Joash.

Joash (841–796) is said to have ruled for forty years and to have been a good king generally, repairing the temple, though he did not remove the high places. Yahweh punished him by delivering Judah into the hands of the Aramean king Hazael (2 Chron. 24:23–24). Despite the theological rationalization, the reference to Aramean dominance of Judah and the name of a known Aramean king are both realistic details.

Amaziah (796–767) had a long reign, but the only important deed attributed to him is the retaking of Elath. As we saw above, however, there are no archaeological data.

Uzziah (783–732) reigned for fifty-two years (he may have ruled with Amaziah for some time—the biblical chronology is not clear), but he gets only seven verses in Kings. He is said to have been struck by Yahweh with leprosy for his sins, so he lived the rest of his days as a recluse "in a separate house." Some scholars connect that reference to the site of Ramat Rachel on the southern outskirts of Jerusalem. It has been excavated, and it does boast royal architecture such as dressed masonry and decorated capitals. Though the site was occupied in this general era, the royal presence was likely not established until the early seventh century.

One possible correlation of text and artifact is often overlooked. It has to do with a great earthquake that the prophet Amos says occurred in the reign of Uzziah (Amos 1:1). The synchronism is unclear, but the earthquake must have occurred about 740 BCE. At both Hazor and Gezer archaeologists have observed stone walls of the eighth century that are severely cracked, tilted, and collapsed. These belong to levels that do not look like destruction layers and are most likely evidence of the earthquake of 740 BCE.

What is striking about the hundred and fifty years of Judean history just covered is not the presence of correlations between the biblical account and archaeological data (there are virtually none), but the sparsity of such connections. The biblical writers and editors were almost entirely oblivious to what was really going on in Judah, preoccupied as they were with the evil doings of king after king. Yet there were a number of sites in the south that saw major building activity in precisely the ninth to eighth centuries BCE, all well documented in numerous excavations.

One thing evident at many sites is that they are heavily fortified in a deliberate plan that can only be the result of the initiative of a centralized administration in Jerusalem, that is, of kings. Yet few of these fortified sites—significant achievements—are mentioned in the text, much less connected with the kings we know in this period.

Mizpah, on the northern outskirts of Jerusalem, has a double city wall, a massive gate, and densely built up domestic and commercial quarters. It could have had a population of one thousand or more. Beersheba is our best example of a well-planned district administrative center. It also has a double (or casemate) city wall and a triple-entryway gate. An oval inner ring road parallels the outer wall all the way around the site. It is noteworthy that the very uniform houses are actually incorporated into the double city wall. That feature (seen also at the other sites) can only be explained if this is a barracks town. Only soldiers, likely conscripts, would have lived with their families in such a perilous situation. Three large storehouses adjoining the gate would have stored adequate provisions for a garrison of several hundred soldiers. A huge underground water system supplemented these provisions.

The near-total silence in the Bible about such major developments in Judah over some 150 years is the best support for our argument here that archaeology is now our primary source for writing any new and more satisfactory histories of ancient Israel and Judah.

Next we come to the reign of Hezekiah (715–687 BCE), arguably Judah's greatest king, and one of the few of whom the biblical writers approved. After they devastated the northern kingdom in 732–722 BCE, it was obvious that the Assyrians would move next to overrun Judah. They mounted a major attack under Sennacherib in 701 BCE. We are fortunate in having three sources for this event, making it perhaps the best documented military campaign in the history of the ancient Near East: the Assyrian annals, the biblical accounts, and extensive excavations at Judean sites.

In the Assyrian annals Sennacherib boasts that he captured forty-six walled towns and "shut up Hezekiah the Judean like a bird in a cage." The latter obviously refers to the prolonged siege of Jerusalem, a typical Assyrian military tactic.

The reference to "forty-six walled towns" is clearly an exaggeration; there are not that many known fortified towns or cities in all Judah. But there are as many as a dozen or so excavated sites that do show heavy destruction layers attributed to this period.

At one of them, Tell Halif, north of Beersheba, the contents of one house destroyed suddenly in 701 BCE were found. The family must have fled shortly before the house was burned. It was a disaster, but one that left behind the contents of the house almost intact—damaged, but nonetheless preserved. Among the dozens of items in the household inventory are numerous storage jars and cooking pots; stone, flint, and metal tools; and several miniature stone altars. Here we get an intimate glimpse into the lives of the "ordinary folk" whom the Hebrew Bible largely ignores. (We will see more of them later.)

An even more horrendous Assyrian destruction is documented at Lachish, a large, heavily fortified site in Judah, second only to Jerusalem in importance. In the late eighth century BCE Lachish was protected by a lower and an upper city wall, with a steep slope between them. A triple-entryway gate with an outer guardroom led into the city, high on the hill. There was a massive palace

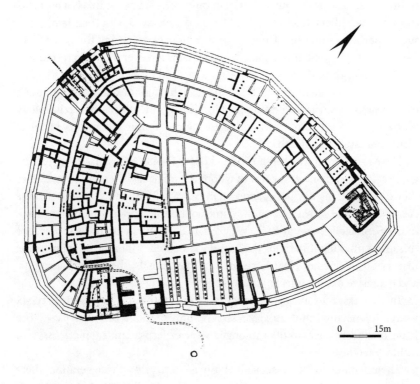

0   15m

Plan of Beersheba, Stratum II

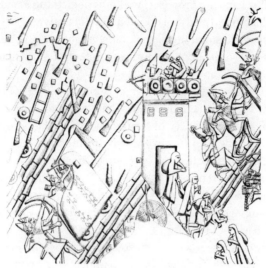

Scene from Sennacherib's reliefs depicting the siege
of Lachish

with its own defense wall and a large courtyard and storehouses. It is the largest
Iron Age building ever found in Israel or Judah.

Despite its formidable defenses, Lachish was destroyed in an enormous con-
flagration. The great water reservoir was found filled with the remains of some
fifteen hundred corpses, people slaughtered when the site was overrun. Lachish
was so badly ruined that the city was never again of much importance.

Sennacherib was so puffed up by his victory at Lachish that he not only
claimed its destruction, he commissioned artists to execute large stone reliefs
picturing the conquest. These reliefs were recovered from the ruins of his
palace at Nineveh and are now in the British Museum. They show Sennacherib on his throne, surrounded by his retainers and with his chariot nearby,
watching the fall of the doomed city. Steep siege ramps have been thrown up,
and ironclad, wheeled battering rams are drawn right up against the city walls.
Arrows and slingstones fly back and forth.

Telescoping several scenes, the Assyrian reliefs depict men, women, and
children streaming from the burning city gates, knapsacks on their back, destined to go into exile. Other scenes show captives impaled on pikes and being
paraded around the city walls. A pile of severed heads looks like watermelons
in a market. Some captives are staked out on the ground, being flayed alive.
Jerusalem would be the next target.

In Jerusalem, Hezekiah was evidently well prepared. Combining the accounts in 2 Kings and 2 Chronicles, we know something about these prepa-rations. Hezekiah refortified and doubled the city walls and strengthened the *millo*; he provisioned storehouses; and, most importantly, he secured Jerusa-lem's always-short water supply by diverting water from the Gihon Spring into the city (see 2 Kgs. 18–20 and 2 Chr. 32).

Here the biblical writers' detailed description of preparations for Sennach-erib's siege has been fully corroborated. There is a secondary city wall found in excavations in the Old City of Jerusalem, called the "Broad Wall" after the wall found among the ruins by those returning from the exile (Neh. 3:8). Also found in the late eighth century at Jerusalem and elsewhere in Judah are dozens of jar handles from large storage jars. They are impressed with a royal signet ring and read: "Belonging to the king." Four different place names give the names of sites where these storage jars were made, filled with provisions, and distributed around Judah.

One of the most remarkable archaeological discoveries ever made in the Holy Land is "Hezekiah's Tunnel." This is an underground rock-cut tunnel that leads from the Gihon Spring in the valley below, under the eastern city wall, and into a reservoir inside the city. The tunnel is some twelve hundred feet long and is so well engineered that water still flows by gravity today. Near the south entrance there was found engraved in the stone wall a royal Hebrew in-scription—the only one we have. Although incomplete or robbed in antiquity (Hezekiah's name is not mentioned), it describes in detail how the engineers began simultaneously at both ends of the tunnel, but managed to connect in the middle almost precisely. Comparative analysis of the elegant script dates it to the late eighth century BCE. This can only have been a royal construction project of Hezekiah. That is striking confirmation of 2 Kings 20:20.

The last important Judean king was Josiah (640–609), whose reign we have discussed above. The most significant event of his reign was, according to the biblical writers, his attempt at reforming the decadent religious cults of his days. That was what earned him the rare approval rating of these writers, who were intent upon restoring the law of Moses. Second Kings 23 details all of Josiah's efforts. But is this account historically reliable, or is it merely another example of a polemical Deuteronomistic agenda?

Many biblical scholars are skeptical that such sweeping reforms ever took place, and few archaeologists have looked critically at the biblical passage in 2 Kings 23. The main inroads into Yahwistic practice that had been made by rival cults include (in order): (1) bringing into the temple pagan vessels made for Baal, his consort Asherah, and "all the hosts of heaven"; women in the temple weaving garments for Asherah; (2) ordaining non-Yahwistic priests;

(4) burning incense to pagan gods and heavenly beings at the high places and elsewhere; and (5) building houses for sodomists (pederasts) near the temple. Josiah responds in turn by (1) dismantling the high places; (2) destroying installations in the Valley of Hinnom where people sacrificed children to the god Molech; (3) destroying the "horses and chariots of the sun" that were in the temple; (4) dismantling the altars in an upper chamber; (5) destroying the Asherah-symbols at high places in Jerusalem and elsewhere; (6) burning the bones from the burials of heretics; (7) killing all the priests of the high places and burning their bones; and (8) forbidding wizards and soothsayers and the images of idols they used. Then the people are commanded to renew the Passover. That's quite a list; but is it a realistic description of actual religious reforms that were carried out, or simply a hit list of zealous reformers?

Today the results of archaeological research can easily explain all of Josiah's reputed reforms. In the "Conclusion" we shall deal more in detail with the popular "folk" religion that was the target. First, the cultic vessels in the temple dedicated to "Baal and Asherah" pose no problem. These deities were a well-known divine pair who had been prominent in the Canaanite pantheon and were still widely revered. "All the hosts of heaven" refers to the lesser gods. The same phrase is often used in the Bible in relation to Yahweh and the heavenly council. The "women weaving vestments for Asherah" in the temple may be difficult. While we already have mention of some implements for worshipping her, now we seem to have something more, a statue of the goddess herself. The Hebrew term often translated as "weavings" or "garments" (*battim*) is obscure. It could mean something like "tents," and we do know of tents attached to sanctuaries, like the tabernacle in the wilderness. So these could be small tent shrines located in or near the temple, providing sanctions for non-Yahwistic rites.

The same is true for burning incense—it was a legitimate form of worshipping in itself, but not when dedicated to other deities, and certainly not when done at "high places." These were old Canaanite hilltop sanctuaries where all sorts of unacceptable things went on. They were rivals of the temple, the only legitimate place for worship (see further the "Conclusion").

The "houses" (or "temples") for "sodomites" pose some problems. The Hebrew term *qedeshim* has been understood as "temple prostitutes" (so the King James Version, "sodomites"). It is a strange sentence, but one once thought to refer to a custom in which sacred prostitutes attracted people (mostly men) to temples with their sexual favors. The notion was that sexual intercourse was thought to be a symbol of one's communion with the gods. It was so argued that "lascivious Canaanite religion" legitimized such atrocious acts in its "fertility cults."

That is all quite fanciful, the misconception of prudish (but fascinated?) interpreters. The Hebrew term comes from a verb meaning "to set aside, consecrate," and it simply refers to people who were dedicated to some religious activity, that is, cult personnel. The term has nothing whatsoever to do with prostitution or sodomy. The only problem here is that these unofficial functionaries should not have been in Yahweh's house at all.

The reference to burning fires in the Valley of Hinnom is interesting. The valley is a deep rift below Jerusalem on the south, leading out from the Dung Gate. It is so called because this is where drain water runs off, and where rubbish is thrown out (still today). Fires often raged there. The Hebrew name for the valley is *gei benei-hinnom*, the "valley of the sons of Hinnom." It came into the Greek translation that early Christians used, the Septuagint, as *gehenna*, the word for "hell"—a fiery place for punishment. So that expression is clear.

The biblical text also calls the valley the "Tophet," where people "made their children pass through the fire to Molech." The reference is to a place of worship in the Phoenician world where people sacrificed infants as burnt offerings to the god Molech. At the Tophet at Carthage in Tunisia, hundreds and hundreds of these child sacrifices have been excavated, many with dedicatory inscriptions.

But did any Israelites actually borrow such horrifying rites? They probably did. Several passages in the Bible refer to kings making a vow by "passing their sons through the fire." This may have been another of the several religious customs belatedly borrowed from the Canaanites in Israelite times—not really a surprise, given what we know about cultural continuity.

The prophet Ezekiel declares of these apostates:

"Your birth and origin are from the land of the Canaanites. Your father was an Amorite, and your mother was a Hittite." (16:3)

That condemnation occurs, significantly, in a passage that also includes a reference to Israelites sacrificing children in fires (Ezek. 16:20, 21).

"Burning incense to the sun, moon, and all the planets" is a clear reference to solar and astral cults. They are well represented in the art of precisely this period, on stamps and signet rings and their impressions.

The "horses and chariots of the sun" in the temple no doubt refers again to worshipping heavenly beings like the sun. Baal is represented as a storm god riding daily across the heavens in his horse-drawn chariot (as is Yahweh, too, the "Cloud Rider").

Josiah had to contend in particular with the goddess Asherah. So he expelled her image (and thus she herself) not only from the temple, but also from the numerous high places in the countryside.

Burning the bones of unofficial priests and other miscreants, having killed them or dug up the remains of those already deceased, requires no explanation. This was the ultimate act of desecration in ancient Israel.

Wizards, magicians, fortune-tellers, and other soothsayers had once been allowed; Saul had called upon a "witch" to summon Samuel's spirit from the grave the night before his death. But later these popular shamans were forbidden, and only levitical priests could perform these functions.

It is noteworthy that before undertaking these unprecedented actions, Josiah called the people together at the temple to read to them from the newly discovered scroll, the "book of the Law." Then, after the purge of forbidden cult practices was complete, Josiah commanded all the people to renew observance of the Passover, which apparently had not been observed for a long time, as specified in the scroll they now had.

In all these actions Josiah had been inspired, and was no doubt being driven on, by Hilkiah the high priest and the scribe Shaphan. Some reforming prophets were also parties to the reformation, like Jeremiah, who were active at just this time. They were also revolutionaries, declaring the "word of Yahweh" at a critical hour in Judah's last days and hearkening back to an original, purer Yahwism at Sinai.

But in fact, that Yahwism was largely a literary construct. What the masses of ordinary folks were actually doing instead was the *real* religion, if numbers count. This was not syncretistic (borrowed from and mixed with Canaanite religion), this was the real stuff. And ideal or not, it is unlikely that Josiah's reforms actually changed much. Folk customs die hard.

Returning to Yahweh and repenting or not, the end was at hand. Prophets and reformers had proclaimed that if Judah would only mend her ways she might be saved; Yahweh would change his mind and spare her. But the fact is that the Babylonians did not know that they were Yahweh's avengers. Suppose the king and high-ranking officials had gone out to meet the Babylonian forces at the border and had informed their commander, "It's okay. We've repented, and Yahweh's forgiven us. You can go home." Would that have made any difference?

We have already summarized the surprisingly brief biblical account above. Jerusalem is sacked and the temple burned by the Babylonians in the spring of 586 BCE. It is certain that many if not most other sites in Judah are similarly destroyed, because the kingdom comes to an absolute end. Large numbers of people are exiled to Babylon, never to return. Only a remnant makes it back to Judah when an edict of the benevolent Persian king, Cyrus, frees them in 535 BCE. After six hundred years, there is no more "Israel" or "Judah." Yahweh disappears. Only the promise of a distant Messiah remains.

One surprising characteristic of the biblical writers who cover the seventh century BCE is the fact that they say very little about the real-life context of their own crowning achievement: the Hebrew Bible. They deal with the reign of Manasseh, who ruled a remarkable fifty-five years (697–642 BCE) in only seventeen verses (2 Kgs. 21:1–17), dismissing him as an apostate and a traitor. In fact, Manasseh was a survivor. He lived during the *pax Assyriaca*, the imposed peace following the Assyrian occupation of Judah after 701 BCE. From Assyrian records we know that Manasseh skillfully steered between extremes, paid tribute, and survived by collaborating with the Assyrians. To be realistic, what else could he have done?

The biblical writers and editors give much more attention to Josiah (640–609 BCE), but almost exclusively to highlight his attempted religious reforms, of which they approved. But of his crucial relations with the Assyrian king Ashurbanipal, whose vassal he was, they say absolutely nothing. Yet Assyria was now in decline, and thus Josiah might have had some opportunity to assert himself, perhaps even to declare independence (though unlikely).

The Bible is inexplicably silent regarding what life in Judah was really like in the seventh century BCE, when many authorities concur that the great Deuteronomistic History was being compiled and edited. In the light of that silence, what we can reconstruct from other sources is the context—the political and social situation that must have done much to shape Israel's epic history stretching from the book of Joshua through Kings.

We now know that for the entire seventh century BCE Judah was a vassal of Assyria, completely subjugated to a brutal empire determined to reach Egypt. Assyria had already obliterated the northern kingdom and deported masses of its population. No one in Judah could have been oblivious to the truth: Judah was next.

In the light of this crisis—the threat of extinction—the challenge of the hour would have been to call urgently for national unity. Specifically, one had to unite the nation by hearkening back to its roots, those ideals that had supposedly guaranteed its survival thus far. Judah would have to reinvent itself or disappear from history.

Precisely that was, of course, the task to which the biblical writers and editors set themselves, and on the basis of a realistic estimate of the precarious situation in Judah. But they never *say* so. Their motive—to save Judah—we can deduce, but they leave us in the dark about what was really going on that moved them. Their eyes are fixed on the heavens, while their world is falling apart. And fall apart it did.

One area where archaeology is our best source for writing more realistic histories of ancient Israel concerns the daily lives of the ordinary people, especially women. We only glimpse them occasionally in the Bible as minor players in the great drama. The elites who wrote the Hebrew Bible—all males—are simply not interested in the masses. (Besides, in their view they are all evil.)

A number of recent books deal with ordinary folk, especially women and their roles, and they are all largely dependent on recent archaeological data. The evidence consists of vernacular four-room "Israelite" courtyard houses of a distinct type that predominate from the settlement horizon of the fall of Jerusalem. Such houses rarely occur elsewhere. They are typical farmhouses that are particularly suited to ancient Israel's rural lifestyle, discussed above.

These dwellings, well known from dozens and dozens of excavations, may house a multigenerational family, or they may be closely grouped together to form a compound serving several such families. In any case, they reflect the biblical ideal of the "house of the father" (Hebrew *bet av*), a patrimonial society and economy that is largely egalitarian and self-sufficient. That is why kingship and authoritarian government were resisted: Yahweh is sovereign.

The existence of such households is sometimes implied in the Bible, as in stories in Judges and Samuel; but there is never any real description. These folk are only part of the larger narrative. One such household and its contents have already been noted in discussing the 701 BCE destruction at Tell Halif in Judah. But without archaeology, we would know next to nothing about the lives of the largely rural classes and village populations, estimated at as much as ninety percent of the total. There were a few large urban centers incorporating the upper classes, but Israel's values remained those of what we would call the proletariat, the economically and socially lower classes, relatively poor and often disadvantaged.

The elites have left us Scripture—enshrining *their* ideals. But archaeology, for better or worse, illuminates the lives of all those anonymous, ordinary people in ancient Israel who had no Bible—"those who sleep in the dust" (Dan. 12:2). They matter too. In particular, archaeology gives back a voice to women, to whose roles we will return presently.

What Is Left and Does It Matter?

In this chapter we have seen how archaeology greatly expands our knowledge of life under the divided monarchy in the ninth to eighth centuries BCE. Beyond the largely political history of the books of Kings, we catch a glimpse of the lives of ordinary people. Many people were, of course, part of the state and its apparatus. And Israel had now become a great nation whose fortunes were interlocked with the imploding geopolitics of the era. The population, however, was still predominantly rural, and rural values prevailed. This remained an agrarian society and economy.

There would have been by now, however, a real sense of both personal and national "Israelite" identity, which would have brought with it a degree of pride. But most people had little news of the larger world beyond gossip. Jerusalem and the temple were far away, the Assyrians and Babylonians even more distant on the horizon. To be sure, in a highly stratified society, some people were doing extremely well. But increased wealth brought corruption. At the top, government officials and religious reformers geared up for invasions by great empires, but all this was not very reassuring. The burdens of nationhood seemed heavy.

While somewhat speculative, since both the Bible and archaeology can seem mute, the portrait here of life during the monarchy accords well with both our sources. This was how it really was to live in an age of great portent and peril. More than the books about kings and their doings, we should look at the great prophets of this era, because they were the realists. Fortunately, we have preserved for us much of their public oracles; but it is archaeology, more than the Bible, that sets the stage on which these spokesmen for Yahweh so eloquently proclaimed their message.

In the north, the prophet Hosea uses the metaphor of a faithless marriage (his own) to declare that Yahweh, as Israel's long-suffering husband, will divorce her and leave her to national ruin. She has committed adultery with false gods. The ruin came, as we have seen, in the form of the Assyrian onslaught in 732–722 BCE.

Amos, a shepherd, excoriates the idle rich who "sell the needy for a pair of sandals" (Amos 8:6). It will be of no use to them when they flee to the national shrines and sanctuaries, for they too are hopelessly corrupt. "Though they climb up to heaven, from there I will bring them down" (Amos 9:2). Yet there may be hope for restoration, if evildoers repent:

> I will restore the fortunes of my people,
> and they shall rebuild the ruined cities and inhabit them;
> they shall plant vineyards and drink their wine. (Amos 9:14)

Micah, living and working in the momentous reign of Hezekiah, also foresees doom. On that day Judah's mountains and valleys will melt like wax

(Mic. 1:4). The chiefs of Israel who build Zion with blood will see it become a heap of ruins (Mic. 3:10–12). But, like Amos, Micah envisions a better time, when the people of Israel will beat their swords into plowshares: "They shall sit under their own vines and own fig trees, and no one shall make them afraid" (Mic. 4:3, 4). This is the old vision of the good life, which remains the inspiration.

It was the great statesman and prophet Isaiah, who counseled Hezekiah during Sennacherib's siege in 701 BCE, who had the most profound insight into Judah's fate. He seems ambivalent as to whether Hezekiah should surrender and survive or whether the siege of Jerusalem would miraculously be lifted. The siege was lifted in the end; but there was no ultimate miracle. Judah was doomed. Yet it is Isaiah's words of promise that were immortalized in Handel's oratorio *Messiah* (even if mistakenly taken to refer to Jesus). Jerusalem will yet be Zion, Yahweh's holy mountain. Isaiah's vision is a worldview that takes in all of Judah's neighbors—Philistia, Aram, Moab, Edom, Egypt, and even distant Assyria.

> Then Yahweh will wipe away the tears from all faces,
> and the disgrace of his people he will take away from all the earth.
>
> (Isa. 25:8)

In Judah's last days, the prophets Jeremiah and Ezekiel struggled with the inexorable Babylonian advance and the certainty that Jerusalem and the temple would be destroyed. How to reconcile that with the centuries-old promise that David's dynasty would last forever? Jeremiah spoke truth to power, and he paid dearly for it. Yet he fled to Egypt and survived, with a few other refugees. Ezekiel also survived the holocaust and lived on to comfort his fellow exiles in Babylon. Like Jeremiah, he was a realist, a prophet of doom. He even acted out the tragedy in his own bizarre, troubled life.

In his *History of Israel*, John Bright says of these figures that "they were men from every walk of life who had felt the compulsion of Yahweh's word and who had often—probably always—come to their vocation through some experience of call."[3]

What archaeology adds to the biblical portrait of the life and times of the great prophets of Israel is *tangibility*. It gives to us a first-hand, real-life grasp of their world, not just spiritually, but in all its materiality. And their vision,

---

3. John Bright, *A History of Israel*, 4th ed. (Louisville: Westminster John Knox, 2000), 264.

while seemingly far-fetched, still resonates with us precisely because it relates not simply to literature, but to life.

Before leaving the prophets, let us look at a few details of their life and work that archaeology illuminates uniquely. Archaeology has supplied a real-life context for many prophetic utterances that were long thought to be vague and therefore lacking real thrust. For example, Amos rails against the idle rich of Samaria who have "built houses of hewn stone" (5:11), "who oppress the poor, who crush the needy" (4:1), who "lie on beds of ivory" (3:15; 6:4). These condemnations are directed precisely at the inhabitants of Samaria. The excavations of the royal quarter of Samaria have clarified these passages by uncovering fine ashlar (chisel-dressed) masonry, numerous fragments of elaborate Phoenician-style carved ivory inlay panels for wooden furniture, and ostraca (potsherds with inked inscriptions) that reveal how a few large estates and wealthy landowners dominated the economy.

Micah denounces the aristocracy who "covet fields, and seize them; and houses, and take them away" (2:2; cf. Isa. 5:8). They accumulate their wealth by falsifying weights and measures so as to defraud ordinary people—"wicked scales and a bag of dishonest weights" (6:11; cf. Amos 8:5). Then the needy can be bought for a pair of sandals (cf. Amos 8:6). Excavations have revealed large, luxurious houses in some cities. More specifically, stone shekel weights for weighing commodities in balances, which should have conformed to national standards, are sometimes too heavy—like "the butcher's thumb on the scales." The shekel sign of these weights resembles the bag or pouch in which they were carried. One biblical reference to a specific weight, carved with the Hebrew word *pym* (1 Sam. 13:21) remained enigmatic until these actual weights inscribed with *pym* came to light, and they weigh about two-thirds of a shekel.

Israel's long history in the divided monarchy—three hundred years—should teach us some lessons, especially if archaeology brings it down to earth a bit. First, we can learn that achieving national destiny is not a simple, automatic trajectory. It is a process, often long and painful, fraught with many difficulties and setbacks. Perhaps Israel was "the chosen people," but there were many other people, their neighbors, who had a similar sense of destiny. Conflicts were thus inevitable, and Israel did not always prevail. Was Israel chosen for other things beside greatness?

Late in the monarchy, and more so in the exile in Babylon, those who wrote the Hebrew Bible and edited it into its final form began to rethink

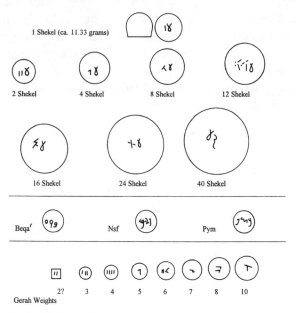

The Judahite shekel-weight system

the doctrine of election. In the latter part of the book of Isaiah, Israel is now envisioned not as exclusive, but rather as inclusive—"a light to the nations" (Hebrew *goyim*). Jerusalem will become the true Zion, a city set on a hill that will draw all peoples to the new Israel. This will be her destiny, her greatness, her eternal heritage. Second, the disastrous end, first of the northern kingdom, and then of the southern kingdom a century later, can teach us that nothing lasts forever, that all good things come to an end. The biblical writers rationalized these disasters by declaring that it was all Israel's fault for abandoning Yahweh. Assyria and Babylon would be instruments of Yahweh's wrath if Israel did not repent. As Isaiah puts it, Yahweh declares: "Ah, Assyria, rod of my anger!" But to be realistic, repentance and renewal would have done nothing to slow, much less to avoid, a tidal wave. Had the people been united around a single deity they might have been able to resist a bit longer, but the end was inevitable.

Finally, we see that again the "good life," especially in an age of uncertainty and loss of values, is that of ordinary families. That would even outlast the nation.

Sociologists often speak about "greater" and "lesser" traditions that shape culture. The former consists of the public lives and deeds of great men, preserved in epic literature. That is history. But there is also a lesser tradition, preserved not necessarily in literature but in cultural memory, in oral traditions, in the lives of ordinary people over a long span of time. It is the latter that archaeology has now brilliantly illuminated in ancient Israel. And that record is history too.

CHAPTER 7

Religion and Cult: How Many Gods?

Religion, however defined, was an essential element of ancient Israelite society, as it was everywhere else in any society that we know of. Yet we have not said much about religion in our chapter-by-chapter treatment of each period. Why the neglect?

There is a reason, and it lies in the fact that the religious situation in each successive era seems to have remained essentially the same. Thus in this final chapter we turn back to the beginning, first to characterize the situation generally. Then we can summarize what little may have changed over time, mainly in the light of the archaeological data, since the biblical texts are not easy to separate out chronologically.

Running like a scarlet thread through the Deuteronomistic History, from Deuteronomy through Kings, and in much of the contemporaneous prophetic literature as well, there is one theme: Israel's obligation to be faithful to the covenant with Yahweh at Sinai. Running parallel to that is another theme: Israel's recurring failure to do so and the consequences that will surely follow. Thus this epic history of the Israelite peoples from the exodus to the end is not simply a history of events, nor does it pretend to be. (There is no Hebrew word for "history" in the Bible.) This is *theocratic* history, history viewed primarily as the acts of Yahweh, Israel's creator and sole deity.

In that sense, the biblical version of Israel's history is an *ideal* history—a portrait not of what Israel actually was, but of what it *should* have been had it conformed to orthodox Yahwism. By that term we mean the religious beliefs and practices of the elites who wrote and edited the Hebrew Bible—right-wing, orthodox, nationalist parties and the literati in Jerusalem. Thus it should come as no surprise that the Bible presents a revisionist history that fails to represent the views and the practices of the majority.

The Hebrew Bible is a minority report. If that fact limits its usefulness for the modern historian, there is some consolation: archaeology today can supply much that is missing. It can also balance the picture by portraying the lives of the majority of the people of Israel, those who never wrote a Bible and could not have read it if they had one. Those people were different, in both their beliefs and practices.

The conflict between two versions of religion underlies the stories in the Deuteronomistic History, particularly in Kings. That is why, despite clinging to their commitment to the *idea* of kings as "Yahweh's anointed ones," the writers denounce every single actual king in the north, and all but two (the reformers Hezekiah and Josiah) in the south. They all "made Israel sin." And the sin is that they forsook Yahweh for other gods, and worse still they led the people into idolatry.

From beginning to end, the biblical writers and editors are specific about what the elements of this apostasy were. Scholars thus draw a contrast: on the one hand there is the orthodox cult, or what may be called "book religion." This is the ideal, institutionalized religion of the Bible. Then there is popular or "folk" religion. The biblical writers condemn the latter, a perversion in their view, and try to call Israel back to an original, purer version—theirs. But their religion was an ideal, almost never the reality, an ideal that they projected back upon a largely imaginary past.

The real religion(s) of the ancients consisted of almost everything that the biblical writers condemned. That was what people were actually doing, and had been doing ever since their ancestors lived in Canaan. To call this family or household religion practiced by the majority a "pagan" religion is not a value judgment, nor does it side with the Bible's condemnation. The word "pagan" derives from Latin *pagus*, "countryside." It comes to denote those untold folk in the rural areas in the Roman period who failed to convert to Christianity when the emperor Constantine declared it an official religion. Most Israelites were similarly rural folk and untutored in the Bible (which they didn't yet have). So if by "authentic" we mean earlier and more widespread, then the religion of ordinary folk—of "pagans"—*was* the more authentic.

We do not have to disparage the biblical view of authentic religion to understand this dichotomy. We do need, however, to see what family and household religion was, what it is that the Bible condemns. First, ordinary religion was often practiced at local "high places." The Hebrew plural term *bamoth* is somewhat vague, but it usually refers to hilltop shrines of some sort, elevated heights obviously being closer to the gods. These sites were often wooded, and the gods were naturally associated with groves of trees as well, flourishing green trees seeming somehow magical in a sparse landscape. At these high places the old Canaanite deities were still viable: the dominant pair, El and his consort Asherah, the parents of the lesser gods; the rival pair, the storm god Baal and his wife/warrior companion Anat; and a host of lesser gods and goddesses.

All this had to do with what has been called (perhaps simplistically) "fertility"—seeing the gods as the source of survival and fruitfulness. These gods must be placated, and their blessings must be secured if one is to survive. Religion is all about *ultimate* concern, and in antiquity generally nothing was more ultimate, more existential, than survival in a perilous world. Only the gods could save one and one's family.

The principal features of the high places are fairly consistent in the biblical portrayal. There were upright stone pillars, denoted by the Hebrew term *matseboth*. Such stones, often quite large, represent deities, or more precisely the sacred ground where a deity has appeared. They had long been venerated, as when Abraham first goes to the "oak of instruction" at Shechem, or when Jacob erects a standing stone to commemorate his vision of Yahweh and the angels at Bethel.

At the high places, and in homes as well, there would have been altars. These were usually low stone platforms on which one could place the food and drink offerings for the gods that were characteristic of both Canaanite and Israelite religions. Thus one secured the blessing of the gods by giving back to them a portion of their bounty, a practice well suited to a rural agricultural society and economy.

The most obvious feature at many high places (and the most odious to the biblical writers) was the presence of an *asherah*. This Hebrew term occurs some forty times in the Hebrew Bible. Often it refers to something that is to be destroyed by being chopped down, cut in pieces, and burned. Therefore, the *asherah* can be a tree, or a treelike symbol (a wooden pole) that represents a goddess—in this case the old Canaanite mother goddess Asherah.

But in a half dozen or so references, the term *asherah* must be read as a personal name that denotes the goddess herself, not merely her symbol. Thus if "Baal and Asherah" are referred to as a pair, as they are (e.g., Judg. 6:28; 2 Kgs. 23:4), the term *Asherah* then must denote the great mother goddess Asherah.

The biblical writers either use the term *asherah* indiscriminately, or else, writing later, they misunderstand it. Or perhaps they are deliberately obscuring the term due to their hostility toward this pagan deity. The confusion is compounded when we note that the translators of the Septuagint, the Greek version of the Hebrew Bible translated ca. 150 BCE, rendered the term *asherah* into Greek as *alsos*, "grove of trees." Thus Josiah is said to have removed the "groves" from the temple in Jerusalem, quite a feat. But the connection of the goddess Asherah to high places with groves of trees is already present in the Hebrew Bible's description of Israel's idolatry. They worship "on every high hill, on all the mountaintops, under every green tree, and under every leafy oak" (Ezek. 6:13; see also Hos. 4:13; Jer. 3:6). That is the ultimate abomination.

It should be noted that the widespread Israelite religions of "hearth and home," even though they are deigned evil in the Hebrew Bible, had many attractions. They represented continuity with the local Canaanite culture, and therefore stability. They required no elaborate and costly temples, no aristocratic priesthood. The family members—partly and maybe principally women—could officiate, along with village elders. They did not need the sanction of a literary tradition; even illiterates could participate.

Above all, these vernacular religious rites did not require theological formulations, like those in the Hebrew Bible. These rites were the stuff of real life. That is why they remained popular, despite the determination of the Yahwistic reformers to stamp them out. And now we understand the reason for the polemics: this was what most people were *actually* doing, from the settlement horizon until the end of the monarchy. It would not have been so vigorously condemned otherwise.

Most biblical scholars now conclude that polytheism—or what some call "poly-Yahwism," *many* versions of Yahwism—was the norm throughout the history of ancient Israel. Not until the destruction of Jerusalem and the temple and the exile, when Israel had finally learned a painful lesson, did monotheism finally emerge triumphant. That monotheism in Scripture, and in practice, is what prevailed in later Judaism, and of course in its offshoot, Christianity.

The stories in the book of Judges describing the situation in Israel's earliest days in Canaan in the twelfth to eleventh centuries BCE should reflect earlier conditions, still remembering experiences in the wilderness wanderings. That would mean that the Sinai covenant with Yahweh would be celebrated in perpetuity, along with the feast of Passover. Furthermore, the elaborate commandments in the books of Numbers and Deuteronomy would have been observed in various rituals. Of course all of this would be made easier and enhanced once a temple in Jerusalem is eventually built. Even so, the absence of any of this orthodox Yahwism in the literature is striking. Even if written down much later, there should have been some oral traditions preserved.

If one looks through the entire book of Judges, the only reference to any Sinai theme seems to be found in the story of the ark of the covenant rest-ing at Shiloh, being captured, then returned. Otherwise, we see only family and household shrines and altars where food and drink offerings are made, mentioning Yahweh, but with nothing said about "reciting the mighty acts of Yahweh." That is the case in the stories of Gideon, Manoah, and Micah. Then there are rites at the "Oak of Shechem," which harkens back not to Sinai, but much earlier to Abraham. Not only this, but in Judges there are clear references to ritual paraphernalia that are presumably forbidden by Yahweh. Micah worships with graven and molten images of deities; there is no mention of Yahweh. He even anoints one of his own sons, a non-Levite, as a priest, and he clothes him with a priestly ephod (the exact meaning of which is unknown).

There is, to be sure, a reference in Joshua to a temple at Shechem. But is it a Canaanite temple, the temple of Baal-berith ("Baal of the covenant"), and not of Yahweh and his covenant (Judg. 9:46)? Compare Joshua 24, where the name of the same building is changed to "the shrine/sanctuary of Yahweh," a nod in the direction of orthodoxy.

All in all, the biblical portrait of religion in the period of the judges is one where the older Canaanite cult, with its multiple deities and fertility motifs, prevails. Yet it is striking that the authors and editors of Judges—stout Yahwists one and all—nowhere condemn this specifically, except to say that these folk can't be blamed. In the Micah story, they explain it all: "In those days there was no king in Israel, but every man did that which was right in his own eyes" (Judg. 17:6).

From the period of the settlement of Israel in Canaan in the twelfth to eleventh centuries BCE, we have only one clear cult site. The "Bull site" is a rural, open-air shrine in the tribal area of Manasseh, in the central hills north of Jerusalem. An Israeli farmer discovered it by chance when he found a well-preserved bronze Zebu bull (thus the site's name) in a field. When the site was excavated it turned out to be a small, one-period shrine featuring a circular stone surrounding wall and a low stone altar. Around the altar were a few potsherds, metal fragments, and remnants of a terracotta offering stand.

The potsherds are typical of known Israelite villages in the vicinity, giving us a date. The bronze bull figurine is the only item of any particular interest. It is almost identical to one found in the 1950s at Hazor, dating to the Canaanite era some two hundred years earlier. It is that one item that gives us a clue as to what was going on here. The old Canaanite high god was El, whose principal epithet was "Bull El" in the many Late Bronze texts that we have.

There were many bull cults in antiquity in and around the Mediterranean world, the bull being widely seen as a symbol of both ferocity and fertility. One thinks of the famous scenes on Cretan frescoes, featuring elaborately coiffured,

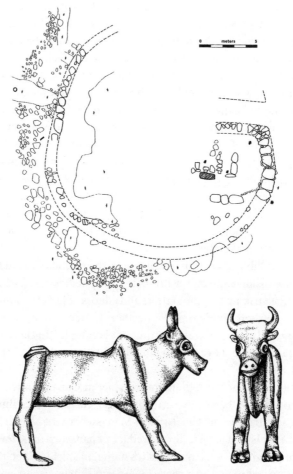

**Twelfth-century BCE bronze bull
and a plan of the site where it was found**

semi-nude jumpers leaping over the backs of bulls. On Cyprus, worshippers were initiated into bull cults at enormous stone altars with horns—the "horns of consecration." The Roman mythraeums were dedicated to a bull god, the novice being initiated by being showered with bull's blood.

It is worth recalling that the Israelites at Sinai set up a golden calf in Moses's absence, even though such things were forbidden. And when Jeroboam inaugurated the offshoot Israelite cult in the north after a civil war, he also erected two golden calves, one at Dan and the other at Bethel on his southern border.

The salient point here is that at the *only* cult place we know in earliest Israel, the cult image is that of a bull—reminiscent not of Yahweh (who has no images), but of his rival, the old Canaanite male deity El. Yet that may not be so surprising if we recall that early Israelite culture and religion stand clearly in the local Canaanite tradition. Furthermore, God has two names in the Hebrew Bible: his personal name, Yahweh, and the name El in many of the older strands of the text, as in Genesis, as the generic term for God. And the name El can occur in the plural, Elohim, as in the creation story. There the gods (*elohim*) say: "Let us make humans in our image, male and female." We will return later to the notion of God(s) as gendered.

One isolated find from the period of the judges is a large terracotta offering stand found in an Israelite house shrine at ʿAi, north of Jerusalem, which was settled after it was erroneously said to have been destroyed by Joshua (above). On top there was a provision for a removable bowl that would have been used for food and drink offerings. Down the cylindrical sides of the stand were windowlike openings, no doubt for burning incense, another familiar custom. But protruding around the bottom are clearly several human feet. Does this reflect someone's foot fetish, or is it an incorporation of the fundamental idea that Yahweh is invisible, as he had said to Moses, who wanted to see him: "I will pass by, and you can see my backside." So one could not actually portray Yahweh; but you could show his feet, as though to declare, "He is here." Thus the second commandment could be honored, if only in the breach.

Religion and cult in the united monarchy during the tenth century BCE, not surprisingly, should have centered around the temple built by Solomon in Jerusalem. All religious practices are to be carried out exclusively there, under the watchful eyes of the levitical priesthood. This is a royal cult. In theory, this form of centralized national cult would have precluded the pagan practices of the period of the judges, when people are in effect excused for doing whatever they pleased, since there was no king, no temple, no authoritative priesthood, so no real blame.

We actually have evidence, however, that few people were worshipping in Jerusalem. In reality, how could they have done? Most people had probably never been to Jerusalem in their whole life. It was a long, difficult, hazardous journey on a donkey's back or on foot. The biblical requirement that all males go to Jerusalem once a year is only the ideal; it could never have been the reality. The Jerusalem temple may have loomed large in the imagination of the biblical writers, but it was peripheral in the lives of ordinary worshippers.

At Tell el-Farʿah (biblical Tirzah, the first capital) a tenth-century-BCE gate shrine was found, featuring a large standing stone (the biblical *matsebah*;

 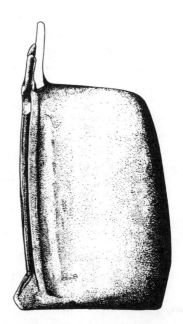

Naos found at Tell el-Far'ah

above) and a stone basin for libation offerings.
Venturing outside the security of a walled town
was exceedingly dangerous in antiquity. If one
were to go out and return safely, an offering
to the gods at the gate would be appropriate.

In addition, other finds at Tell el-Far'ah
include figurines of nude females (to which
we will return) and a terracotta temple model,
called a *naos* after the inner sanctum of Greek
temples. The model has two columns flanking the doorway (like the Solomonic temple).
Other *naoi* have windows around the sides
and back; and, standing in the entrance, a
nude female figure. She closely resembles the
female figurines already seen elsewhere at Tell
el-Far'ah.

Terracotta female figurine

These *naos* temple models have largely been ignored by scholars. At one
time they were rare, but we now have an increasing number from both sides of
the Jordan. Who are these nude females? The answer may be found at another

cult site. At Taʻanach, near Megiddo on the south side of the Jezreel valley in lower Galilee, archaeologists have found an intact village shrine of the tenth century BCE. Among its many features are altars, basins, hearths, and cooking pots for preparing food offerings; a bowl full of astragali, or sheep-goat knuckle bones, often used in various magical rites such as casting lots and fortune-telling; and a large stone basin for processing olive oil, used for liturgical rites such as anointing the hair of worshippers.

But one item found was a tall, rectangular, terracotta offering stand—the most remarkable piece of ancient Israelite art ever found. Below an opening at the top for a removable bowl are four registers modeled in bold bas-relief. From top down they depict a winged quadruped flanked by two trees (a familiar motif in Canaanite art); two lions with rampant goats nibbling the branches of a tree between them (another Canaanite theme); two more cherubs (lions with human heads) and an empty doorway between them (for whom?); and on the bottom, another nude female figure, grasping two lions by the ears. What is going on with this model? Surely not something having to do with the contemporary temple in Jerusalem!

Elsewhere in the Levant, in both texts and

Taʻanach offering stand

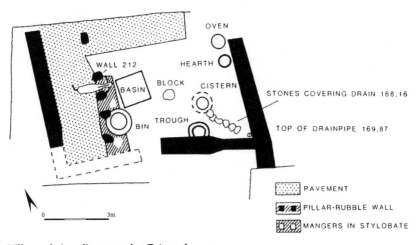

Village shrine discovered at Taʻanach

Reconstruction of the cult installation at Tel Dan

pictorial representations, we have ample evidence that Asherah, whom we have already met, was widely known as the "Lion Lady." So here is the great goddess, forbidden or not. Soon we will meet her again, in her other guises.

Perhaps because of the accidents of discovery, the ninth century BCE is not well represented. There is, however, an elaborate temple and sacred precinct found at Tel Dan on the northern border of the kingdom of Israel. It may have begun in the ninth century BCE, and it continued into the eighth and seventh centuries BCE.

The Tel Dan cult installation includes a large high place (Hebrew *bamah*) with an adjoining three-room shrine featuring a stone altar and iron shovels for clearing away burnt offerings. Nearby was an olive oil press, a large four-horned altar, and a smaller broken one.

Elsewhere there were bronze bowls, a bronze priestly scepter head, terracotta offering stands, and both female and male figurines. Obviously the Tel Dan cult installation functioned as a full-fledged religious complex with its own priests—precisely what the Jerusalem religious establishment condemns. The Dan temple precinct would have served the ruling class, but ordinary folk as well.

In the eighth century BCE we have even more conclusive evidence for non-establishment expressions of religion. At Arad, near Beersheba, we have the only actual Israelite temple ever found. It is comparable to the Jerusalem temple in plan, with three rooms. In the inner room (the "Holy of Holies") are two standing stones or *matseboth*. There are also two small, stylized, four-horned altars flanking the entrance into the inner chamber, probably for incense. In the middle room, a courtyard, there is a large stone altar, at the front of which were found offering bowls and a small bronze lion. An inscribed Hebrew ostracon refers to the "house (temple) of Yahweh." Other

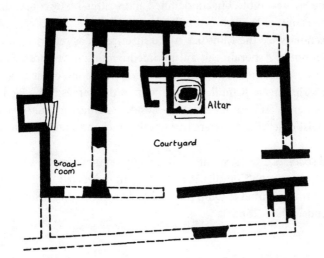

Plan of the Arad temple

inscriptions give the names of priestly families like those in Jerusalem. This temple served mostly the garrison stationed there.

The Arad temple has been cited as evidence for cult reforms such as those purportedly carried out by Hezekiah and Josiah. The two standing stones, the taller one perhaps representing Yahweh and the smaller one representing Asherah, were not found as they now appear in the archaeologists' restoration. They had been carefully laid down under the floor and subsequently plastered over at a later date. A third standing stone was also found there. These alterations do indeed look like a deliberate attempt at reform. If so, they reflect an effort to purge this local temple by removing the principal objects of worship, perhaps as described in the reforms of Hezekiah.

Far away in the Sinai desert, at an isolated hilltop along the caravan routes, we have an eighth-century-BCE fort at the site of Kuntillet 'Ajrud. It is a rectangular building with casemate walls and corner towers. In the two-chamber gateway there was a shrine with low, plastered benches and rear chambers that are called *favissae*, places for discarded sacred objects. The excavators found Hebrew inscriptions all around on the plastered walls as well as other inscriptions and painted scenes on large storage jars.

One scene depicts two figures of Bes, an Egyptian good-luck deity; a bare-breasted female figure seated on a lion throne, perhaps Asherah (?); and a Hebrew inscription that is a blessing formula. It reads in part "I bless you by Yahweh of Samaria and by his Asherah." As we have seen, Asherah is remembered in the Hebrew Bible, but condemned and written off by construing her as the consort, not of Yahweh, but of Baal.

Some scholars see the Kuntillet 'Ajrud inscription as referring only to a treelike symbol of Asherah. But an unforced reading of *Asherah* as a personal name, as sometimes in the Hebrew Bible, seems more convincing. Other Hebrew inscriptions at Kuntillet 'Ajrud contain the names of El, Baal, Yahweh, and Asherah. At a minimum, the wayside sanctuary at Kuntillet 'Ajrud was polytheistic, serving travelers from both Israel and Judah (as shown by the pottery).

Biblical scholars often say that "archaeology is mute; show us some *texts.*" Now, in addition to the Kuntillet 'Ajrud inscription, we have another eighth-century text from Khirbet el-Qom (biblical Makkedah), west of Hebron in the southern Judean hills. It reads:

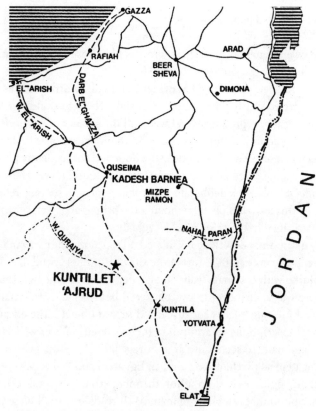

Location of Kuntillet 'Ajrud in the Sinai

For Uriyahu the governor, his inscription.
Blessed be Uriyahu by Yahweh.
From his enemies he has been saved
by his Asherah.
(written) by Oniyahu

Uriyahu is a good biblical Hebrew name meaning "Yahweh is my light." And we have already met Asherah. Some scholars are still reluctant to name her, so they read "saved by Yahweh and his treelike symbol"—as though Yahweh needed help. Again, the more credible reading is "saved by his (that is, Yahweh's) Asherah." Here, then, Yahweh and his consort are united, as the Canaanite deities were, in a context of blessing.

The el-Qom inscription comes from a large, multigenerational family cemetery that reflects local traditions of worship for some two centuries in Judah. And the cult there appears to be polytheistic, although Yahweh may nevertheless predominate.

Some scholars who are uneasy about such religious pluralism get around the problem by arguing that these "pagan" practices were confined to the countryside, where ordinary people were isolated and not well informed. But we have evidence of similar nonconformist practices right in Jerusalem—the spiritual center—and they date from the seventh century BCE, when the prophets were warning of doom for those who abandoned Yahweh.

Painted figures and inscription at Kuntillet 'Ajrud

Judean and Phoenician terracotta pillar figurines

Within the shadow of the Temple Mount there was found a large cave complex that was either a cult installation or a repository for discarded cult objects. The cave contained hundreds of pottery vessels such as bowls and lamps, as well as dozens of clay female figurines. In a house on the Ophel hill, within sight of the Temple Mount, there was found a house shrine with small stone altars, several kinds of offering vessels, and fragments of animal figurines.

Another cave, a burial in the Valley of Hinnom, produced two tiny rolled-up silver amulets, designed to be worn around the neck, no doubt as good-luck charms. When carefully unrolled, one had the name of Yahweh in an inscription that reads almost identically to the famous priestly blessing in Numbers 6:24: "May Yahweh bless you and keep you . . ." Here we have preserved for us the oldest surviving fragment of biblical text, at least five centuries older than the oldest Dead Sea scrolls. And Scripture is not being read; in effect it is worn as magic. That is "folk religion."

The archaeological evidence summarized above (and there is much more) is fairly recent, but it has spawned an array of works on the alternate versions of ancient Israelite religious *practice.* These are often in sharp contrast to the "ideal" version enshrined in the Hebrew Bible, that is, the orthodox *theology.*

Yet this contrast should not be surprising, since there are significant differences between clergy and laity in nearly all religions. The two parties may be legitimate, both in theory and in practice. In the case of ancient Israel, however, we are not dealing with "idolatry" (as the biblical writers insist) as much as with a *broader understanding* of deity, one that without archaeology we would scarcely have known about.

If we pause to think about it, the language and imagery about God in the Bible is almost exclusively male. But why should that be? Is it because men wrote the Bible, and they naturally saw God in their own image? So God is the divine warrior who fights aggressively against Israel's enemies, like a real man would do. But where is God the nurturer, the comforter? Perhaps women in ancient Israel simply experienced Yahweh, Israel's god, in their *own* ways. For them, he brought blessing in the form of children to be reared and cherished, while the men were off doing politics and war. Asherah was not a pagan deity, and the female figurines were not idols, but rather symbols of her procreative powers. Put simply, the biblical writers were chauvinists who denigrated women. But as archaeology now shows us, women had real power, not only in the religion of "hearth and home," but sometimes even in the public arena. And at home, they were the *real* priests.

For many women, their role was primarily to enlarge and preserve the family and its heritage by bearing and rearing children—a formidable task in antiquity. One may argue that they should have had careers, but there were no opportunities then. Thus the female figurines, which were probably to be found in every house, may be best understood, as one scholar put it, as "prayers in clay."

In one view, however, they were simply *symbols* of a great mother, not actual representations of the goddess Asherah. That is, they symbolized mortal women, not deities. They survived as votive statuettes—stand-ins for the worshipper in her absence from the shrine. But in the houses where these figurines are most often found, the women were not absent; they were constantly present. And we must never say "only" a symbol. Without the deity perceived as standing behind the symbol, it would have had no power. The star of David, the cross, the crescent—these are all symbols. Powerful?

What Is Left and Does It Matter?

Suggesting lessons to be drawn from our archaeologically based portrait of ancient Israel may be the most difficult and controversial of all. Many people in

Postmodernism and the Western Cultural Tradition

"Postmodernism" is a widespread but often obscure or misunderstood intellectual and cultural phenomenon. As a movement or school of thought, it is notoriously difficult to define, since it begins by denying the possibility of any rational
definitions. It is more feasible to define postmodernism not by what it is for but
by what it is against: modernism.

"Modernism" may be defined essentially as what is often called the Western
cultural tradition. This was a widespread revolution in thinking beginning with
the Renaissance and its aftermath in the fourteenth to sixteenth centuries, reach-
ing its full flowering in the eighteenth century. The revolution affected numerous fields of inquiry such as philosophy, theology, literature, art and aesthetics;
perceptions of the natural world and the universe; popular culture; and culture
in general. The hallmarks of the Enlightenment enterprise were reason, science,
the dignity and freedom of the individual, humanism (often secular), positivism,
and the notion of progress in history. Somewhat later, notions of orderly states
("democracy") and economic promise ("capitalism") came to be part of the Enlightenment view. Postmodernism opposes and negates all this.

the Western or Enlightenment cultural tradition—whether Jews, Christians, or
humanists—side with the biblical writers and their view of history and moral
values, not with secular interpretations, such as those here, based largely on
archaeology. Fundamentalists declare: "God said it. I believe it. That settles it."
Liberals want to preserve some moral traditions in the Bible, but they may not
be able to see beyond a literal reading of the text.

Here we try to find a middle way, not one based on rigid theological propo-
sitions (archaeology cannot provide that and should not try). Our way depends
on broad, general observations grounded in nature and in human nature—but
contained in principle in the biblical stories when read in a "real-life" context.
As we have seen, such metaphorical or allegorical readings are found already
in the Hebrew Bible itself, and they have found equal place in the long history
of textual interpretation.

A critical observer may protest that all of the "lessons" derived here from
a new reading of the Bible could have been learned just as easily without the
Bible. After all, other religions besides Judaism and Christianity have advo-
cated nearly identical moral values. And many secular humanists would want
to occupy a similar high ground.

Nevertheless, most of us in the Western cultural tradition have derived our
values *initially* from the biblical worldview. Whether we could sustain those

values without that historical underpinning remains to be seen. Dismantling a tradition, as postmodernists have attempted, is easy, but replacing it is very difficult.

The fundamental lesson to be learned is that God (or, if you wish, the gods) is greater than all our human language and imagery. We cannot put God in a box. The biblical writers knew that, the rabbis knew that, the church fathers knew that, and now we can know that too.

Conclusion

This book has been based on the premise that archaeology as a new interpretive tool now enables us to read the Hebrew Bible with greater understanding—and hope—by bringing it down to earth as it were. We can make the Bible more credible by seeing beyond its few elite authors to the lives of the masses of people who were also part of the biblical world. These are those, to turn a phrase from the book of Daniel, "who sleep in the dust" (12:2). Archaeology gives them a voice. We can learn by listening. If we do not learn from the past, as the philosopher Santayana says, we are doomed to repeat its mistakes.

Finally, doing the truth—the truth we know—is more important than arguing about it; practice defines religion better than theology. Moreover, it is possible to be a deeply spiritual person without subscribing to any particular creed, or affiliating with one or another religious institution. We are not gods. It is enough to be *fully human.*

The great philosopher Alfred North Whitehead once remarked that "religion is what the individual does with his solitariness."[1] That means having moral courage—not waiting for another world, but doing what is right in this world, here and now.

The Bible, read not only with a critical and well-stocked mind, but also with the eyes of faith, can help us to do that. And archaeology may be our best friend in the task. It is our latest tool, and thus far one of the best. Archaeology can only grow more useful as excavations progress and new information comes to light. We have nothing to fear from that exploration—on the contrary, everything to hope for.

---

1. Alfred North Whitehead, *Religion in the Making*, 2nd ed. (New York: Fordham University Press, 1996), 6.

Above all, this book has argued that from a sophisticated reading of the Bible and of Israel's past we can take new courage to face *our* time. In his book *Why Religion Matters,* the eminent historian of religion Huston Smith affirms that there are two kinds of truth:

> On the one hand are the truths of knowledge as these are derived from science and from discursive, empirically grounded reason. On the other hand are the truths that faith, religious experience, morality, meaning, and value put forward. The latter are not grounded in knowledge. They arise out of a blend of feeling, intuition, ethical action, communal convention, folk tradition, and mystical experience.[2]

The Nobel Prize–winning poet Czeslaw Milosz tells us:

> On one side there is luminosity, trust, faith, the beauty of the earth; on the other side, darkness, doubt, unbelief, the cruelty of the earth, the capacity of people to do evil. When I write, the first side is true; when I do not write, the second is.[3]

Here we have tried to write what to us seems true.

The moral lessons that we have drawn from each chapter on ancient Israel's history, as reconstructed by recent archaeological evidence, may seem somewhat minimalistic. Indeed, one might argue that in this case, our "revised Bible" may no longer be necessary. We might as well dismiss the Bible as mostly legendary, and thus irrelevant for questions of moral values.

To respond to this challenge, let us first acknowledge that it is obvious that we cannot insist that the Hebrew Bible is essential to formulating and defending moral values. After all, it has been available to us only for the past three thousand years or so, out of more than one hundred thousand years of human history, the mere blink of an eye. And even so, our Bible, part of the Western cultural tradition, has never been or ever will be the Scripture of the vast majority of people on this planet. What about all the countless millions of others? Are they devoid of moral and ethical standards? Surely not.

Secondly, nearly all of the moral lessons derived here from a modified reading of the Hebrew Bible could just as easily be derived from any num-

---

2. Huston Smith, *Why Religion Matters*, reprint ed. (San Francisco, HarperOne, 2009), 100.

3. Quoted in Smith, *Why Religion Matters*, 24.

ber of other religions, from such various forms as moral philosophy, secular humanism, or even from universal human experience and common sense. Take, for instance, what many would regard (mistakenly) as the heart of the Bible and Judeo-Christian religion: the Ten Commandments. Subtract the few commands peculiar to Judaism—the prohibition of images, the keeping of the Sabbath—and nearly all the others are universal and timeless. Who would not universally commend loyalty to one's parents, respect for all human life, faithfulness in marriage, not coveting or stealing other people's property, not lying? Even the commandments, apparently relevant only to Judaism, to not speaking frivolously about god(s) and to take one day a week for rest and rejuvenation make good sense.

Finally, we should note that a literal transliteration of the first commandment—"You shall have no other gods before me"—would read "have no other gods *in my face*" (Hebrew *al-panay*). That is a candid acknowledgment that there are indeed other gods besides Israel's national god Yahweh; but you shall not offend him by "throwing them up in his face."

All this leaves as unique to Judaism (not, of course, to Christianity) only one commandment: the prohibition against making images of god, i.e., the principle of aniconism. Most other religions depend heavily on icons of many sorts, or symbols, visible "signs" that point to invisible and spiritual realities. Yet even that commandment, while seemingly unreasonable, makes sense. It reflects a nearly universal perception of deity; the gods *are* indeed invisible as spiritual powers, so no image could do them justice.

If, as we have concluded here, the Hebrew Bible is not an essential basis for moral values, why continue to venerate it? The only defensible argument is that this is for most of us in the modern Western world *our* tradition, our authority for asserting the values by which we have chosen to live and which define our culture. Surely there is room for other traditions, especially if they affirm similar values.

In conclusion, is archaeology, in bringing to light a new "Israel," burying the Bible? Not at all. It is bringing the Bible as well as ancient Israel into a new and brighter light. It enables truly sophisticated, critical, modern readers to find things that they can still believe and defend in reading the Bible—things for which they need to offer no apologies.

Suggested Readings

Here are some suggested further readings for nonspecialists who desire more documentation. Most of these works are, of necessity, scholarly or semi-scholarly discussions. For convenience, they are organized by topic.

Many readers, however, may simply wish to consult my earlier work, a more extensive companion volume to this one: *Beyond the Texts: An Archaeological Portrait of Ancient Israel and Judah* (Atlanta: SBL Press, 2017). This is a massive work (747 pages) with hundreds of references, and every topic addressed here can be found there with a more detailed discussion and references.

Dictionaries and Encyclopedias

Freedman, D. N., ed. *Anchor Bible Dictionary*. 6 vols. New York: Doubleday, 1992.

Meyers, E. M., ed. *The Oxford Encyclopedia of Archaeology in the Near East*. 5 vols. New York: Oxford University Press, 1998.

Arnold, B. T., and H. G. M. Williamson, eds. *Dictionary of the Old Testament Historical Books: A Compendium of Contemporary Biblical Scholarship*. Downers Grove, IL: InterVarsity Press, 2005.

Master, D. M., ed. *The Oxford Encyclopedia of the Bible and Archaeology*. New York: Oxford University Press, 2013.

Atlases

Rainey, A. F., and R. S. Notley, eds. *The Sacred Bridge: Carta's Atlas of the Biblical World*. Jerusalem: Carta, 2006.

Chronology

Galil, G. *The Chronology of the Kings of Israel and Judah*. Leiden: Brill, 1996.

Levy, T. E., and T. Highman, eds. *The Bible and Radiocarbon Dating: Archaeology, Text and Science*. London: Equinox, 2005.

Biblical Commentary Series

Anchor Bible Commentary Series. New York: Doubleday.

History and Old Testament Scholarship

Rogerson, J. W. *Old Testament Criticism in the Nineteenth Century: England and Germany*. Philadelphia: Fortress, 1985.

Barr, J. *History and Ideology in the Old Testament: Biblical Studies at the End of a Millennium*. Oxford: Oxford University Press, 2000.

Collins, J. J. *The Bible After Babel: Historical Criticism in a Postmodern Age*. Grand Rapids: Eerdmans, 2005.

Handbooks for Old Testament Studies

Friedman, R. E. *Who Wrote the Bible?* Englewood Cliffs, NJ: Prentice Hall, 1987.

Coogan, M. D., ed. *The Oxford History of the Biblical World*. Oxford: Oxford University Press, 2001.

Coogan, M. D., ed. *The Old Testament: A Historical and Literary Introduction to the Hebrew Scriptures*. Oxford: Oxford University Press, 2001.

Schniedewind, W. M. *How the Bible Became a Book: The Textualization of Ancient Israel*. Cambridge: Cambridge University Press, 2004.

Matthews, V. H. *Studying the Ancient Israelites: A Guide to Sources and Methods*. Grand Rapids: Baker Academic, 2007.

Moore, M. B., and B. E. Kelle. *Biblical History and Israel's Past: The Changing Study of the Bible and History*. Grand Rapids: Eerdmans, 2011.

Ebeling, J., J. E. Wright, M. Elliot, and P. V. M. Flesher, eds. *The Old Testament in Archaeology and History*. Waco, TX: Baylor University Press, 2017.

Suggested Readings

Historiography

Brettler, M. L. *The Creation of History in Ancient Israel*. London: Routledge, 1995.

Dever, W. G. *What Did the Biblical Writers Know and When Did They Know It? What Archaeology Can Tell Us about the Reality of Ancient Israel*. Grand Rapids: Eerdmans, 2001.

Kofoed, J. B. *Text and History: Historiography and the Study of the Biblical Texts*. Winona Lake, IN: Eisenbrauns, 2005.

Williamson, H. G. M., ed. *Understanding the History of Ancient Israel*. Oxford: Oxford University Press, 2007.

Grabbe, L. L. *Ancient Israel: What Do We Know and How Do We Know It?* London: T&T Clark, 2007.

Barstad, H. M. *History and the Hebrew Bible: Studies in Ancient Israelite and Ancient Near Eastern Historiography*. Tübingen: Mohr Siebeck, 2008.

The "Biblical Archaeology" Movement

Silberman, N. A. *Digging for God and Country: Archaeology and the Secret Struggle for the Holy Land*. New York: Knopf, 1982.

Moorey, P. R. S. *A Century of Biblical Archaeology*. Cambridge: Lutterworth, 1991.

Dever, W. G. "Archaeology, Syro-Palestinian and Biblical." In *Anchor Bible Dictionary*, edited by D. N. Freedman, 1:354–67. New York: Doubleday, 1992.

Davis, T. W. *Shifting Sands: The Rise and Fall of Biblical Archaeology*. Oxford: Oxford University Press, 2004.

Hoffmeier, J. A., and A. Millard, eds. *The Future of Biblical Archaeology: Reassessing Methodologies and Assumptions*. Grand Rapids: Eerdmans, 2004.

Levy, T. E., ed. *Historical Biblical Archaeology and the Future: The New Pragmatism*. London: Equinox, 2010.

Dever, W. G. "A Critique of Biblical Archaeology: History and Interpretation." In *The Old Testament in Archaeology and History*, edited by J. Ebeling, J. E. Wright, M. Elliot, and P. V. M. Flesher, 141–57. Waco, TX: Baylor University Press, 2017.

Postmodernism

Gress, D. *From Plato to NATO: The Idea of the West and Its Opponents*. New York: Free Press, 1998.

Lemert, C. *Postmodernism Is Not What You Think.* Oxford: Blackwell, 1997.

Windschuttle, K. *The Killing of History: How Literary Critics and Social Theorists Are Murdering Our Past.* New York: Free Press, 1997.

Handbooks—"Biblical" and Levantine Archaeology

Mazar, A. *Archaeology of the Land of the Bible: 10,000–586 BCE.* New York: Doubleday, 1990.

Ben-Tor, A., ed. *The Archaeology of Ancient Israel.* New Haven: Yale University Press, 1992.

Levy, T. E., ed. *The Archaeology of Society in the Holy Land.* London: Leicester University Press, 1995.

Stern, E., ed. *New Encyclopedia of Archaeological Excavations in the Holy Land,* vols. 1–5. Jerusalem: Israel Exploration Society, 1993; 2008.

Other Histories of Ancient Israel

Miller, J. M., and J. H. Hayes. *A History of Ancient Israel and Judah.* Philadelphia: Westminster, 2006.

Mazar, A., and I. Finkelstein. *The Quest for the Historical Israel: Debating Archaeology and the History of Early Israel,* edited by B. B. Schmidt. Atlanta: SBL Press, 2007.

Shanks, H., ed. *Ancient Israel: From Abraham to the Roman Destruction of the Temple.* 3rd ed. Washington, DC: Biblical Archaeology Society, 2011.

Dever, W. G. *Beyond the Texts: An Archaeological Portrait of Ancient Israel and Judah.* Atlanta: SBL Press, 2017.

Early Israel, ca. 1200–1000 BCE

Dever, W. G. *Who Were the Early Israelites and Where Did They Come From?* Grand Rapids: Eerdmans, 2003.

Killebrew, A. E. *Biblical Peoples and Ethnicity: An Archaeological Study of Egyptians, Canaanites, Philistines, and Early Israel, 1300–1100 BCE.* Atlanta: SBL Press, 2005.

Faust, A. *Israel's Ethnogenesis: Settlement, Interaction, Expansion and Resistance.* London: Equinox, 2006.

Suggested Readings

Religions of Ancient Israel

Olyan, S. *Asherah and the Cult of Yahweh in Israel*. Atlanta: SBL Press, 1988.

Nakhai, B. A. *Archaeology and the Religions of Canaan and Israel*. Boston: American Schools of Oriental Research, 2001.

Becking, B., M. Dijkstra, M. C. A. Korpel, and K. K. H. Vriezen. *Only One God? Monotheism in Ancient Israel and the Veneration of the Goddess Asherah*. Sheffield: Sheffield Academic, 2001.

Zevit, Z. *The Religions of Ancient Israel: A Parallelactic Approach*. London: Continuum, 2001.

Dever, W. G. *Did God Have a Wife? Archaeology and Folk Religion in Ancient Israel*. Grand Rapids: Eerdmans, 2005.

Hess, R. S. *Israelite Religions: An Archaeological and Biblical Survey*. Grand Rapids: Baker Academic, 2007.

Bodel, J., and S. M. Olyan, eds. *Household and Family Religion in Antiquity*. Malden, MA: Blackwell, 2008.

Yasur-Landau, A., J. R. Ebeling, and L. B. Mazow, eds. *Household Archaeology in Ancient Israel and Beyond*. Leiden: Brill, 2011.

Albertz, R., and R. Schmitt. *Family and Household Religion in Ancient Israel and the Levant*. Winona Lake, IN: Eisenbrauns, 2012.

Albertz, R., B. A. Nakhai, S. M. Olyan, and R. Schmitt, eds. *Family and Household Religion: Toward a Synthesis of Old Testament Studies, Archaeology, Epigraphy, and Cultural Studies*. Winona Lake, IN: Eisenbrauns, 2014.

Daily Life

Hopkins, D. *The Highlands of Canaan: Agricultural Life in the Early Iron Age*. Sheffield: Almond Press, 1985.

Borowski, D. *Every Living Thing: Daily Use of Animals in Ancient Israel*. London: AltaMira, 1998.

King, P. J., and L. E. Stager. *Life in Biblical Israel*. Louisville: Westminster John Knox, 2001.

De Geus, C. H. J. *Towns in Ancient Israel and the Southern Levant*. Leuven: Peeters, 2003.

MacDonald, N. *What Did the Ancient Israelites Eat? Diet in Biblical Times*. Winona Lake, IN: Eisenbrauns, 2008.

Dever, W. G. *The Lives of Ordinary People in Ancient Israel: Where Archaeology and the Bible Intersect*. Grand Rapids: Eerdmans, 2012.

Faust, A. *The Archaeology of Society in the Iron Age II.* Winona Lake, IN: Eisenbrauns, 2012.

Women's Lives in Ancient Israel

Ackerman, S. *Warrior, Dancer, Seductress, Queen: Women in Judges and Biblical Israel.* New York: Doubleday, 1998.

Meyers, C. *Households and Holiness: The Religious Culture of Israelite Women.* Minneapolis: Fortress, 2005.

Nakhai, B. A., ed. *The World of Women in the Ancient and Classical Near East.* Cambridge: Cambridge Scholars, 2008.

Ebeling, J. R. *Women's Lives in Biblical Times.* London: T&T Clark, 2010.

Writing and Literacy

McCarter, P. K. *Ancient Inscriptions: Voices from the Biblical World.* Washington, DC: Biblical Archaeology Society, 1996.

Ahituv, S. *Echoes from the Past: Hebrew and Cognate Inscriptions from the Biblical Period.* Jerusalem: Carta, 2008.

Rollston, C. A. *Writing and Literacy in the World of Ancient Israel: Epigraphic Evidence from the Iron Age.* Atlanta: SBL Press, 2010.

Evangelical Works, to the Right

Miller, A. R., J. K. Hoffmeier, and D. W. Baker, eds. *Faith, Tradition, and History: Old Testament Historiography in Its Near Eastern Context.* Winona Lake, IN: Eisenbrauns, 1994.

Baker, D. W., and B. T. Arnold. *The Face of Old Testament Studies: A Survey of Contemporary Approaches.* Grand Rapids: Baker Books, 1999.

Kitchen, K. A. *On the Reliability of the Old Testament.* Grand Rapids: Eerdmans, 2003.

Provan, I. W., V. P. Long, and T. Longman III. *A Biblical History of Israel.* Louisville: Westminster John Knox, 2003.

Hess, R. S., G. A. Klingbeil, and P. J. Ray Jr., eds. *Critical Issues in Early Israelite History.* Winona Lake, IN: Eisenbrauns, 2008.

Hoffmeier, J. K., and D. R. Magary, eds. *Do Historical Matters Matter to Faith?*

A Critical Appraisal of Modern and Postmodern Approaches to Scripture. Wheaton, IL: Crossway, 2012.

Liberal Approaches to the Bible and Faith

Steinberg, M. *Basic Judaism*. New York: Harcourt, 1947.

Spong, J. S. *Rescuing the Bible from Fundamentalism: A Bishop Rethinks the Meaning of Scripture*. San Francisco: HarperSanFrancisco, 1991.

Levenson, J. D. "Why Jews Are Not Interested in Biblical Theology." Pp. 33–61 in *The Hebrew Bible, the Old Testament, and Historical Criticism*. Louisville: Westminster John Knox, 1993.

Smith, H. *Why Religion Matters: The Fate of the Human Spirit in an Age of Disbelief*. San Francisco: HarperSanFrancisco, 1991.

Trudeau, R. *Bible Stories for Skeptics: Why You Don't Have to Believe in the Supernatural to Be a Christian—or a Jew*. North Easton, MA: Chad Brown Publishing, 2013.

Sources for Illustrations

p. 85   **Solomon's temple footprint**
Courtesy Yosef Garfinkel; used with permission

p. 87   **Six-chamber gates of Iron Age Israel**
Courtesy Zeev Herzog, Tel Aviv University; used with permission;
following Zeev Herzog, *Archaeology of the City: Urban Planning in
Ancient Israel and Its Social Implications* (Tel Aviv: Emery and Claire
Yass Archaeology Press, 1997), 266

p. 112   **Plan of Beersheba, Stratum II**
Courtesy Zeev Herzog, Tel Aviv University; used with permission;
following Zeev Herzog, *Archaeology of the City: Urban Planning in
Ancient Israel and Its Social Implications* (Tel Aviv: Emery and Claire
Yass Archaeology Press, 1997), figure 5.31

p. 113   **Scene from Sennacherib's reliefs depicting the siege of Lachish**
Courtesy David Ussishkin; drawing by Judith Dekel; used with permission; following David Ussishkin, *The Conquest of Lachish by Sennacherib* (Tel Aviv: Tel Aviv University Press, 1982), plate 86

p. 123   **The Judahite shekel-weight system**
Courtesy Raz Kletter; used with permission; following Raz Kletter, "The Inscribed Weights of the Kingdom of Judah" (*Tel Aviv* 18
[1990]:121–63), figure 6

p. 130   **Twelfth-century BCE bronze bull and a plan of the site where it was
found**
Courtesy Amihai Mazar; used with permission; following Amihai Mazar, "The 'Bull Site': An Iron Age I Open Air Cult Place (*Bulletin of the
American Schools of Oriental Research* 247 [1982]:27–42), figures 2, 5

p. 132   ***Naos* found at Tell el-Farʿah**
Following Alain Chambon, *Tell el-Farʿah: L'âge du fer* (Paris: Editions
recherche sur les civilisations, 1984), plate 66

p. 132   **Terracotta female figurine**
Following Alain Chambon, *Tell el-Farʿah: L'âge du fer* (Paris: Editions
recherche sur les civilisations, 1984), plate 66

p. 133   Ta'anach offering stand
Following K. H. J. Vriezen, "Archaeological Traces of Cult in Ancient Israel," pp. 45–80 in *Only One God? Monotheism in Ancient Israel and the Veneration of the Goddess Asherah*, ed. M. C. A. Korpel and K. H. J. Vriezen (Sheffield: Sheffield Academic Press, 2001), figure 12

p. 133   Village shrine discovered at Ta'anach
Following Paul W. Lapp, "The 1963 Excavations at Ta'anek" (*Bulletin of the American Schools of Oriental Research* 173 [1964]:4–44), figure 12

p. 134   Reconstruction of the cult installation at Tel Dan
Following Avraham Biran, *Biblical Dan* (Jerusalem: Israel Exploration Society, 1994), 319

p. 135   Plan of the Arad temple
Courtesy Othmar Keel; used with permission; following Othmar Keel, *The Symbolism of the Biblical World: Ancient Near Eastern Iconography and the Book of Psalms* (Winona Lake, IN: Eisenbrauns, 1997), figure 170

p. 136   Location of Kuntillet 'Ajrud in the Sinai
Following Ze'ev Meshel, *Kuntillet 'Ajrud: A Religious Centre from the Time of the Judean Monarchy on the Border of Sinai* (Jerusalem: Israel Museum, 1978)

p. 137   Painted figures and inscription at Kuntillet 'Ajrud
Following Ze'ev Meshel, *Kuntillet 'Ajrud: A Religious Centre from the Time of the Judean Monarchy on the Border of Sinai* (Jerusalem: Israel Museum, 1978)

p. 138   Judean and Phoenician terracotta pillar figurines
Following K. H. J. Vriezen, "Archaeological Traces of Cult in Ancient Israel," pp. 45–80 in *Only One God? Monotheism in Ancient Israel and the Veneration of the Goddess Asherah*, ed. M. C. A. Korpel and K. H. J. Vriezen (Sheffield: Sheffield Academic Press, 2001), figure 13

Index